Audition Speeches

for 6~16 year olds

To Jennifer, Jamie, Amieth and Thomas

Audition Speeches

for 6 ~ 16 year olds

Jean Marlow

A & C Black • London

First published in 2000
by A & C Black (Publishers) Limited
35 Bedford Row, London WC1R 4JH

ISBN 0-7136-5109-1

A CIP catalogue record for this book is available from the
British Library.

Typeset in 10 on 12pt Palatino
Printed and bound in Great Britain by Creative Print and
Design (Wales), Ebbw Vale

Jean Marlow

Frankly, I cannot think of a better person than Jean Marlow to be given the task of finding speeches for young actors.

From her early years when she played an astonishing sea lion in an impro for the Royal Court Theatre, until more recently when she was the leading Hen – 'Mrs Short-and-Long' – in *A Fox and His Drum* at the Unicorn Children's Theatre, she has retained a sense of fun – a sense of fun that stood her in good stead when she worked in Weekly Rep. Did they really have to learn a new play every week? (You can if the devil drives.)

Later, she became a presenter on commercial radio, interviewing pop stars and playing hits from the 'Top Twenty'. She has also worked in many comedy series on television, and written and acted in films for the Children's Film Foundation. She played 'Mrs Jiniwin' in the Disney mini-series production of *The Old Curiosity Shop* and was 'Mrs Bunn' in *Whizziwig* – for Carlton Television.

She is Co-Director of The Actors' Theatre School and is the author of *Audition Speeches For All Ages and Accents*, *Classical Audition Speeches* and *Duologues For All Accents and Ages*.

Eamonn Jones
Founder Director
The Actors' Theatre School

Contents

List of Audition Speeches

Girls 6-8

(1) *Alice's Adventures in Wonderland* . . . . . Lewis Carroll 18
(2) *Have You Seen Zandile?* . . . . Gcina Mhlope 20
    Maralin Vanrenen
    Thembi Mtshali
(3) *The Lion, the Witch and the Wardrobe* . . C.S. Lewis 22
    Dramatised by Adrian Mitchell
(4) *The Magic Mirror* . . . . E.C. Brereton 24
(5) *The Mystery of the Pie and the Patty Pan* Beatrix Potter 26
    Dramatised by Rona Laurie
(6) *Tom Kitten and His Friends* . . . . Beatrix Potter 28
    Dramatised by Adrian Mitchell
(7) *Whizziwig* . . . . Malorie Blackman . 30
(8) *The Wild Swans* . . . . Hans Andersen . . . 32
    Dramatised by Rona Laurie

Boys 6-8

(1) *Beauty and the Beast* . . . . Nicholas Stuart Gray 34
(2) *Cider with Rosie* . . . . Laurie Lee 36
    Dramatised by James Roose-Evans
(3) *The Giraffe and the Pelly and Me* . . . . . . Roald Dahl 38
    Dramatised by Vicky Ireland
(4) *Hansel and Gretel* . . . . Jean Marlow 40
(5) *The Red Balloon* . . . . Anthony Clark . . . 42
(6) *The Snow Queen* . . . . Jean Marlow 44
(7) *Toad of Toad Hall* . . . . Kenneth Grahame 46
    Dramatised by A.A. Milne
(8) *The Witches* . . . . Roald Dahl 48
    Adapted by David Wood

Girls 14-16

Boys 14-16

Acknowledgements

I would like to say thank you to the actors, directors, playwrights, casting directors, teachers, agents and organisations who have helped me with this book, and especially:

Carol Schroder, Brian Schwartz and the Offstage Bookshop, Jennifer Whelan, Jamie Dolan, Amieth Yogarajah, Tay Brandon, Kevin Daly, John Higgins, Kasia Coleman, Kieran Coleman and the students from The Actors' Theatre School, Rona Laurie, Paul Todd, Jill Murphy, Gillian Diamond, Jaye Lewis, Heather Stoney, Maggie Lunn, Helen Curtin, Barbara Roberts, Katherine Adamenko, James Hogan of Oberon Books, Hilary Lissenden, Elly Crichton Stuart of Unicorn Children's Theatre, Samantha Iles of Alan Brodie Representatives, Samuel French, my Co-Director Eamonn Jones, the publishers A & C Black and my editors, Tesni Hollands and Katie Taylor.

Preface

Finding over fifty audition speeches for yonger actors has been a bit of an adventure – like taking on a dare. Could I actually find that many and would they be any good? Fortunately, I was helped by a group of young actors who not only suggested plays, films and books that they had seen or read, but tried out every single speech I selected to see if it worked. Some of these selections they used in their London Academy (LAMDA) or Guildhall Acting Examinations, or in end-of-term shows.

Each speech has its own introduction, with a brief outline of the story so far and a description of the character. All the speeches have been put together with children in mind, but I hope that parents and older actors will enjoy them and that teachers, in particular, will find them useful. The age-groups range from six to sixteen, but I could as easily have said from six to sixty as so many of these speeches are suitable for adults as well – especially those who work in Children's Theatre. 'Mole' in *Toad of Toad Hall* is in the six to eight age-group; but 'Moley' was played by actor Richard Goolden on stage and radio for over forty years. He was still playing the part in the West End at the age of eighty-five!

At the beginning of this book I have invited professional actors, playwrights, directors and casting directors to talk about their experiences working in children's theatre and television, and in some cases to give useful tips about auditioning.

It's been enormous fun searching out these speeches and talking to children's writers who have been so helpful and enthusiastic and care such a lot about their work. My last great 'find' was the adaptation of *The Worst Witch*. There were two children with me at the time, and I wish everyone could have heard the cries of, 'Here comes the Worst Witch!' as the script came sliding out of my fax machine – and the book was complete.

Introduction

IN FRONT OF THE WHOLE CLASS

Everybody remembers the first time they had to 'stand up and do something' in public: Mums, Dads, teachers, actors, pop stars, the Prime Minister – everybody. It could be reciting a poem you only learnt the night before in front of the whole class, singing a song at a party or saying your 'one line' at the end-of-term play. For some, it's a magic moment; others feel awkward or just plain scared.

I remember playing 'Miss Muffet' in a show given by my dancing school in a big hall over the top of the Express Dairy in the High Street. I was four. My Auntie had made me a special dress and I had a little blue bowl with gold stars on it. The class sang 'Little Miss Muffet' and I had to sit there eating my 'curds and whey'. But there was no spoon to eat them with and no spider. I felt really silly – I couldn't even join in the song because I didn't know the words. At the end, when the audience applauded half-heartedly, I joined in and applauded myself – banging my hands together as hard as I could because it was the only thing I knew how to do! 'Miss Muffet' taught me two important things about performing in public. Be sure you know your words, and always remember to check your 'props' before you go on stage – i.e. the spider my dancing teacher forgot to lower down from the ceiling, and the spoon I left behind me in the dressing-room.

Props

There are lots of opportunities at the beginning of this book for the very youngest of actors to learn to use props, whether real or imaginary. In *Alice in Wonderland*, Alice picks up the gloves and fan left by the White Rabbit and begins to fan herself. Toto in *The Red Balloon* has a 'kitten' in a box; Zandile waves her 'stick' when she pretends to be the School Teacher talking to the flowers in her grandmother's garden; and Mikey the baby dragon in *Beauty and the Beast* chews on his 'chicken-bone'.

'Learn the wordies'

A friend of mine once found himself sitting opposite a famous old actor on a tube train. He felt he had to speak to him, so he leaned across from his seat and said, 'I am a young actor just starting out in the theatre. What is the secret of your success? Can you give me any advice?' The great man replied, 'Learn the wordies, my boy! Learn the wordies!'

It's surprising how many people can't be bothered to 'learn the wordies' properly yet hope to get away with it! If I'd learnt the words of 'Little Miss Muffet' I could have sat there singing away happily with the rest of the class. Know your words. It's important. Just 'sort of' knowing them with your Mum hearing you through at home isn't enough. Know them inside-out and you'll feel a lot more confident.

'Can you hear me at the back!'
Some of you may already be attending stage school either full or part-time, and are not only entering for drama examinations but also being sent for theatre or television auditions. I'm sure that you've already learnt that the most important thing of all is: *Voice*. Can you be heard? If no-one hears you there is no point in doing anything. 'Street cred' is no good in a big space like a hall or theatre. If you don't say the beginnings or ends of the words clearly they just float off into a big 'nothing'. You don't have to sound 'posh' – just make sure everyone can hear you. Always play to the back of the theatre and the front will take care of itself. Or, as my teacher used to say, 'Remember little deaf old auntie sitting in the back row.' Don't rush your words. Most people speak too fast. They want to get the whole thing over as quickly as possible, so it all becomes a gabble. At last season's drama auditions a small girl came running out of the exam room screaming, 'Pig!' (I'm sure we've all felt like doing that at some time or other). The secretary explained very kindly to her parents that the examiner *had* to fail her. She had obviously tried to get her speeches over as quickly as she could and had gone far too fast!

Read the play
Although I've tried to give as much information as possible about individual speeches, you still need to read the play. Most plays can be borrowed from the library, and if the one you want isn't in stock they will order it for you or send you to another library that *has* got a copy. It is essential to find out as much as you can about your character. Ask yourself the following questions: What do the other characters say or think about my character? What does my

character say or think about them? What does my character think about himself or herself? When was he or she born and in what period? Who is my character talking to – a friend or an enemy, a teacher or a parent? Make a list of your answers. These are the clues to your character and the key that can unlock the scene for you.

IMPROVISATION, THEATRE GAMES AND TEXT

Improvisation and theatre games are important. They help to build up your confidence and develop imagination and self-expression. They are also great fun. Very often you are asked to improvise – that is, to make up a scene or create a situation – at an audition; but it is just as important to work on 'text' – the *written* words of a play or script – and have at least one good speech learnt that you can produce at a moment's notice!

A casting director complained recently about the number of young actors who are sent to see her without having anything they can perform, not even a short poem. 'An 11-year-old boy came in for an audition. He had no speech prepared and couldn't remember anything he had done. I suggested perhaps he could recite a nursery rhyme. I'll never forget having to prompt him on 'Humpty Dumpty'.'

SIGHT-READING

If you are auditioning for theatre, films, television or radio – yes, even commercials – you are very likely to be asked to 'read'. This doesn't just mean burying your head in the script and mumbling away; it means trying to give the director or casting director an idea of the sort of performance you will give if you get the part. Don't let yourself be hurried or rushed into reading straightaway. Ask if you can have a minute to look through the lines. Then, when you are ready to begin, remember to try to look up as much as you can. This 'lifts the words off the page' and brings your performance to life.

Sight-reading takes practise, and there are lots of good speeches in this book to practise on. Reading aloud like this is also a very good way of finding a speech that you feel happy performing. It doesn't necessarily have to be in your own age-group.

A NOTE FOR TEACHERS AND PARENTS OF YOUNGER STUDENTS

Age-groups

As far as possible I have divided the speeches in this book into age-groups that I think can manage the demands of the particular text. However, these groups do not always match the actual ages of the characters. 'Albert the Mudlark' in *In Service* is described as very young and very small and so of course is the 'Dodger' in *Oliver Twist*, but both these speeches would be too difficult for most students in the six to eight age-group. 'Ernie' in *Ernie's Incredible Illucinations* is in the eleven to thirteen age-group, but my nine-year-old student, Jamie, loves this piece and is excellent when he becomes 'the boxing commentator'. Jennifer is also nine, but her favourite is the 'Grand High Witch' from *The Witches* and she's absolutely determined to use it for her next acting exam. So much depends on individual students, how advanced they are and what they like doing most!

Older age-groups

The speeches in the fourteen to sixteen age-group really come into the category of 'Young Adult' and would also suit students auditioning for drama schools and colleges.

Length of speeches

These selections are just about the right length for most examinations or auditions, unless there is a two-minute time limit specified; in that case they would need to be cut by perhaps a third. Some of the speeches in the six to eight age-group are a little long, but this is because I didn't want to shorten them and spoil the story! There is no reason why they shouldn't be cut. 'Tabitha' in *Tom Kitten and His Friends* can easily finish her speech when she tells her kittens not to 'have anything to do with the Puddle-Ducks', and 'Duchess', the dog in *The Mystery of the Pie and the Patty-Pan* could finish on the line, 'I really couldn't eat a mouse pie.'

CHILDREN'S THEATRE

The majority of speeches in this book are taken from plays written for children and young people: *The Lion, the Witch and the Wardrobe*, *The See-Saw Tree* and *The Wild Swans*, among many others. Alan Ayckbourn, Artistic Director of The Stephen Joseph Theatre,

Scarborough and one of our busiest and most popular playwrights and directors, has this to say about the importance of children's theatre:

'I immensely enjoy writing plays for children, or really for what I prefer to call the 'family' audience, because it's probably as hard if not harder than writing for adults. You have to be more aware. Children won't lie to you – they judge you immediately. They can get bored very quickly. Adults are polite people normally and if something is a little boring, they'll sit and watch it and think, 'Well, it'll get more interesting in a minute.' But children just go, 'Boring!' and turn round and talk to their friends. All the things that matter in any sort of theatre matter twice as much for children. Good story, good dialogue, characters you are interested in. My imagination really catches fire sometimes! To write for such an audience sharpens your playwriting skills no end. It's affected my adult work, I know. In fact, one such play, *Wildest Dreams* – quite a frightening play – is in one sense entirely a children's play. I'd never have written it if I hadn't experienced the thrills and spills of writing for the younger audience. The shame in this country, of course, is how little importance is attached to children's theatre. It's appallingly underfunded – the companies that do exist providing quality work all year round survive on a shoestring. There are many excellent writers producing scripts for children, as is apparent from this book, but there should be many more. But how can there be when they receive precious little monetary reward and hardly any critical acknowledgement?

Young people are the theatre-goers of tomorrow, but if they're never given the chance to see exciting, innovative and imaginative theatre in their childhood, how can they develop an interest in watching plays in their adulthood? If we're not careful, they will be lost forever to television, cinema and all those special effects. They will never have experienced the joy of watching something 'handmade' especially for them in one particular place on one particular day. That's what the 'liveness' of theatre is about and what we have got to *keep* alive.'

About Auditioning

It's always interesting, and often useful, to hear about young actors getting their first professional job – sometimes from an end-of-year showcase and sometimes from an interview or audition. And so I've asked two actors who began their careers when they were still at school, to talk about how they got their first 'breaks'.

France Cuka, a Royal Shakespeare and Royal National Theatre player, tells us how she became a child star on the radio.

'It was the long summer holidays. I was twelve, and bored, so I wrote to the BBC, offering them my services. I told them that I had had elocution and acting lessons, my singing voice had a range of three octaves (it was true at the time), and that I could also produce a light tenor voice if required. I was convinced that they really needed me, so I was a little miffed when I got a reply asking if my letter was meant to be taken seriously. I answered that indeed it was, and some time later I was asked to audition for *Children's Hour*. This programme went on every day from 5.00–6.00 p.m., and had short plays, stories and chats for young people. It was very popular.

The first thing I did for them was a serial of an American family going west in a covered wagon. I played the whiney youngest daughter forever saying, "It's not fair" in a high, shrill voice and generally being a pain in the neck. I also took a tiny part in episode one, of the baby brother. On reaching episode four we found that my two parts had a scene together, so I did a scene with myself!

I did *Children's Hour* through the rest of my schooldays, despite continually having to see the Headmistress to be asked when I was going to give up this "nonsense", and through my time at drama school as well. They always paid me the same, three guineas. No wonder they used me, I was dead cheap!

Later, while in a hit play in the West End, they offered me the lead in a Saturday Night Theatre, at the same money. My agent demanded a great deal more, to get the astonished answer, "She always took it before!"'

Margo Selby – 'Julie Corrigan' in BBC Television's *Grange Hill* – was trained at the Sylvia Young School and played in the National Theatre's production of *Cat on a Hot Tin Roof*. Margo has also appeared in *The Bill, Eastenders*, and played the lead and sang the title song in *Flying Dream* – a children's film about dinosaurs.

'When I was little – before I started acting – I used to get bored and was often very naughty. I would spend hours singing songs from musicals, and used to pretend that I had played the lead in the film of *Annie*. "I know I look different now," I'd say, "but that's the camera for you, and it *was* filmed a couple of years ago!" I would tell everybody this. I was only eight at the time, and I actually thought I had them fooled. Yes, I was very precocious. Being sent to stage school at the age of nine was a dream come true, and I was surrounded by loads of children who had the same passion for performing as me.

I remember my audition for *Grange Hill* very clearly. I walked into the room and fell flat on my face. I then stood up and asked in a giggle, "Do you want me with or without my glasses?" I wasn't shy and I looked the auditioners straight in the eyes. I think this helped me, apart from the fact that I looked right for the part of the school "victim". I was a short, round redhead with glasses – plenty of scope for the bullies!

In nearly all my auditions I have had to read scripts that I hadn't seen before for more than about five minutes. I soon realised that it was essential to be able to read really well. This is important because it allows your character and acting skills to come through in a relaxed and "real" way. I can remember auditioning alongside children who were having difficulties reading the script. They may have been fantastic on screen, but their reading stifled their chances of proving this. The other thing I always found important to keep in mind, was if you are asked to try the part in a different way, be sure to make a point of presenting a *big contrast*. It shows that you are open to direction and can listen and react well with the director.

Smile and have confidence. Good luck!'

WHAT ARE DIRECTORS AND CASTING DIRECTORS LOOKING FOR?
Who are the people you are likely to meet when you audition for
theatre, films, television, radio or commercials? They can be casting
directors, producers, directors or writers – or, in the case of
commercials, advertising agents and their clients. Most important
of all, what are they looking for? Most young actors I've talked to
say it would be really helpful if they could have some advice from
the auditioners themselves, as well as perhaps a few tips on the
'do's and don'ts' of auditioning.

Edward Wilson, Director of the National Youth Theatre, has this
advice to give:

'Auditioning is for some, possibly the most terrifying thing they
ever have to do – worse than a visit to the dentist, or being
chased by a shark!

Unfortunately it's rarely possible to give your best in a state of
extreme nervousness. I think the most important frame of mind
for anyone auditioning is to genuinely enjoy the piece you're
performing and try to convey your own enjoyment to the person
who is auditioning you. Always be as confident as you possibly
can about knowing the words, because the fear of drying up is in
nine cases out of ten the root cause of nervousness in the first
place. So study properly!

Never go along to an audition laden down with costumes or
props. Nothing is more boring and time-consuming for an auditioner than to have to wait whilst someone either dresses up for
the part or arranges an entire furnished room around themselves
before they can even begin to perform their piece. None of this is
necessary and it certainly won't put the auditioner in a good
frame of mind. Similarly, very few auditioners like to be spoken
at, or involved in some way with your performance. It makes it
impossible to observe what you are doing properly. So focus
your attention elsewhere.

Above all remember that whilst it might be a very important
thing to succeed in an audition, it is *not* a matter of life and death.
So enjoy the experience and you'll probably achieve more
success.'

Award-winning television script writer Richard Carpenter, remem-
bered for his *Catweazle* series and more recently *Robin of Sherwood,*

The Borrowers, and *The Scarlet Pimpernel,* started out as an actor. He has strong words to say about auditions and auditioning:

'I used to hate auditions, because I always thought of all the others that had auditioned before me. And I used to feel sorry for the people holding the auditions. How bored they must get – especially if it's the same piece over and over again. "What," I used to think, "are they looking for? Good acting? Something out of the ordinary? Someone who looks like me? Or someone who doesn't?" Trouble is, you don't really ever know. And whoever sent you may have got it wrong. They may be looking for someone older. Or younger. Or taller or shorter. And there's not a lot you can do about that. There's the famous story of the playwright who sent an actor friend of his to an audition for one of his plays. "I've written the part for you," he told him. The actor was bald but he had a very nice wig which he wore for the audition. The director called out to him from the darkness that they were looking for someone bald. Quick as a flash the actor removed his wig. There was a pause. Then the director's voice floated up to him over the footlights. "Er, yes," he said, "but I don't see you *playing* it bald."

So remember this: however good you are – however well you do your audition – it they don't want you, you won't get the part. And it won't be your fault.'

A producer or director is just as anxious to cast the right actor for the part as you are to get the job. Producer and director Neville Green, responsible for the ever popular *Whizziwig* series for Carlton TV, has also produced *Mike and Angelo, Poltergeist,* and the award-winning film, *Never Rest.* He explains the problems of casting and talks about working with children in television.

'It's a headache. It's a heartache. It's a joy. Just a few of the emotions and physical conditions one experiences when working on productions for children and with children.

It's a headache; caused when you can't seem to find, identify, or cast the right child actor for a part in a production after having interviewed, smiled and chatted with what seems like hundreds of children (probably in reality twenty to thirty at the most) – all bright, enthusiastic and intelligent but not one of them that seems suitable for the part.

The heartache; caused by having to reject and turn down children for reasons that are very often nothing to do with them

11

or their ability, but more to do with one's own sense of believing what the part and character should be. No matter how a rejection is said, instantly at the audition – or more usually through their agent – you can still sense the hurt. One can only hope that the maxim, "children are resilient and will bounce back" is the truth.

It's a joy; is pretty obvious. The right child with the right personality has been found and will be a joy to work with.

Working with children is also exceedingly taxing. They are very enthusiastic, energetic and very excited about the production, and they are very interested in all aspects of the technical and creative side of productions. Because of the advent of television and more recently computers, they have a greater concept and awareness of how film and television work and are made, so their questions and interest are much more intensive and knowledgeable. This keeps a director on his toes and up to scratch with the latest electronic and digital effects and techniques. An answer to their questions of, "Er, well, this is an, er, thing that does that, er, good isn't it!" will not satisfy their quest for knowledge.'

Richard Callanan is a producer and director who has specialised in children's drama. His credits include: *Adam's Family Tree*, *Little Lord Fauntleroy*, and *Maid Marian and Her Merry Men*. He was Executive Producer of children's drama at the BBC from 1988 to 1996.

TEN DONT'S FOR AUDITIONS

(1) Don't dress for the part
It's tempting, but it will usually be seen as 'naff'. Working clothes are best – the kind that you can happily rehearse in and that will give you freedom of movement. Wear comfortable shoes too – three-inch high-heels for girls are rarely a good idea. (If you think it might be a good idea, you can always bring them in a bag.) Girls who know it's a costume drama may want to wear a skirt rather than jeans or leggings, but make it a comfortable skirt that you can move in if you are asked to.

(2) Don't audition with your mouth full
Most adults hate chewing-gum. They feel insulted if you talk to them while you chew and it never (well hardly ever) fits with any part you are looking for.

(3) Don't insist on talking too much

Those auditioning you want to get to know you and what you think. So when they ask you a question they hope for more than 'Yes', 'No' and 'Boring'. Don't go to the other extreme either – don't keep on telling the story of your last holiday in Marbella. If you are being auditioned with other kids at the same time, don't hog the spotlight – make sure you don't try to dominate.

(4) Don't fight with other children waiting with you

Waiting for auditions can be very tedious and uncomfortable. The room where you will be asked to wait will probably not be a proper waiting room. It might be overheated and over-crowded. Tempers can get edgy. Resist the temptation to snap at someone waiting with you; they may be rivals, but they can't help it. And try not to sulk if you think things are going badly. Bad behaviour as you wait may be noticed and give you a reputation of being difficult.

(5) Don't flirt with the director

This is a message for everyone who auditions – of both sexes, and any age. Directors (or good directors, anyway) are not interested in flirting. For them auditions are a difficult and demanding process. The success or failure of their project may depend on doing it well. Flirting is not funny or clever. And remember there is usually more than one person involved in casting; a producer, for example, who sees you flirt with a director is unlikely to be impressed.

(6) Don't let your mother, father or 'minder' bully you

Controlling your 'minder' is never more important than at audition. If they are seen to be too pushy it will count against you. Of course, they must feel free to be able to ask questions; but even if they do have to wait around longer than expected, try and get them to keep smiling and not complain out loud.

(7) Don't wait until you are called to go to the loo

Yes, it happens! Kids could be waiting for an hour for their turn, and then – just as they get called in to audition – they ask to go to the loo! Producers and directors like to think of themselves as very busy people so make sure you go before you are called.

(8) Don't hide

The director and his team want to see you. If you are in a group, don't go behind other people, flee to the back of the area or turn your back. It may be natural to the action some of the time but make sure you don't do it continuously.

(9) Don't cover your eyes with your hair
The eyes are the focus of communication. If your eyes cannot be seen when you turn sideways you are losing a major means of expression, so make sure your eyes can always be seen – both of them if possible. (Girls with long hair that wear it up may have another problem. It may make you look older or too sophisticated. If you do wear your hair up, make sure you can let it down easily if asked.)

(10) Don't boast about your dad or mum
It's *you* who are trying to get a part, not your parents. It's you who has to be impressive, not them. So don't say, 'My dad is the drummer in Spiky Sausage.' The likely reply you will get is, 'So what?'

So – now you know!   (JM)

Barbara Roberts, Children's Casting Director for the Royal Shakespeare Company, Stratford-upon-Avon, has this to say about auditioning.

'When I am auditioning here at the Royal Shakespeare Theatre, I usually organise some kind of group warm-up before seeing everyone individually. It helps to break the ice a little, and also gives us a chance to watch such things as movement, etc. in a more relaxed atmosphere.

In the audition itself we are looking for confidence above all – if you are confident you can get away with anything! (Well, almost!) Be as natural as you can and avoid being "stagey".

It is quite useful to have a couple of audition pieces learnt already, then to polish one up when you have an actual audition. A well-rehearsed audition piece stands out from the rest; it shows in your performance that you have taken the time and effort to work on it.

I know how nervous some of you will be, but remember you will have a very short time to show us what you are capable of. Try and put your nerves on hold and enjoy the experience. Make the most of it, and above all, go for it!

Lots of luck.'

Carol Schroder, LLAM is an Examiner for the London Academy of Music and Dramatic Art (LAMDA) and an experienced teacher of drama and performing arts. She has written several textbooks.

'All children enjoy acting. In this new collection of audition speeches for children, there is a delightful variety of suitable material. Teachers will find that these scenes meet the requirements of many performing arts courses and in particular the LAMDA examinations.

As a teacher I enjoyed the inclusion of some familiar characters for very young children and also the adaptations from well-loved books. In all the selections the characters are clearly defined and the scenes are imaginative, which will encourage acting skills.

Writers working in the theatre today are also represented by some stimulating and challenging scenes for both boys and girls. All the texts chosen give opportunities for young actors to explore character, movement, voice and use of space.

As an Examiner I commend this inventive collection of material. I am sure it will prove to be a useful resource book for young performers and their teachers, leading to some creative and successful performances.'

Audition
Speeches

Alice
(Aged 7)

Alice's Adventures in Wonderland

Lewis Carroll

ALICE had been feeling very sleepy, sitting beside her older sister on a grassy bank with absolutely nothing to do, when she saw a White Rabbit, dressed in a waistcoat and pocket-watch, go hurrying past her. She followed the Rabbit, who disappeared behind a bush and into a large rabbit-hole. ALICE went tumbling down after him, and that was the beginning of her adventures in Wonderland.

In this scene ALICE is in a long, low hallway. She has eaten a cake marked, 'Eat me' picked out in currants, and has grown so big that she is unable to get through the little door that leads to Wonderland. She begins to cry and turns to see the White Rabbit, this time splendidly dressed, carrying a pair of white gloves and a fan. When he sees ALICE he drops the gloves and fan and scuttles away. ALICE picks them up and starts to fan herself as she speaks.

Published by Macmillan Publishers Ltd., London

ALICE

Dear, dear! How queer everything is to-day! And yesterday things went on just as usual. I wonder if I've been changed in the night? Let me think: *was* I the same when I got up this morning? I almost think I can remember feeling a little different. But if I'm not the same, the next question is, Who in the world am I? Ah, *that's* the great puzzle! . . . I'm sure I'm not Ada, for her hair goes in such long ringlets, and mine doesn't go in ringlets at all; and I'm sure I can't be Mabel, for I know all sorts of things, and she, oh! she knows such a very little! Besides, *she's* she, and *I'm* I, and – oh dear, how puzzling it all is! I'll try if I know all the things I used to know. Let me see: four times five is twelve, and four times six is thirteen, and four times seven is – oh dear! I shall never get to twenty at that rate! . . . I must have been changed for Mabel! I'll try and say '*How doth the little –*'

> How doth the little crocodile
> Improve his shining tail,
> And pour the waters of the Nile
> On every golden scale!
> How cheerfully he seems to grin,
> How neatly spread his claws,
> And welcomes little fishes in,
> With gently smiling jaws!

I'm sure those are not the right words . . . I must be Mabel, after all, and I shall have to go and live in that poky little house, and have next to no toys to play with and oh! ever so many lessons to learn! No, I've made up my mind about it; if I'm Mabel, I'll stay down here! It'll be no use their putting their heads down and saying 'Come up again, dear!' I shall only look up and say 'Who am I, then? Tell me that first, and then, if I like being that person, I'll come up: if not, I'll stay down here till I'm somebody else' – but, oh dear! . . . I do wish they *would* put their heads down! I am so *very* tired of being all alone here!

Zandile
(Black South African – aged 8)

Have You Seen Zandile?

Gcina Mhlophe, Maralin Vanrenen and Thembi Mtshali

First performed at the Market Theatre, Johannesburg in 1986 and also as part of the Edinburgh Festival at the Traverse Theatre in 1987. It is set in the sixties and is based on Gcina Mhlophe's own life. ZANDILE lives with her grandmother in Durban, a bright child who dreams of growing up to become a teacher – until her world is turned upside down when she is kidnapped by her natural mother and expected to conform to the ways of life in the harsh, rural Transkei homeland. In this scene ZANDILE is only eight years old. She is in her grandmother's garden speaking to the flowers as if they are a class of children and she is their teacher. She has a small stick in her hand.

Published by Heinemann, USA and Methuen, UK

ZANDILE

Ho ho ho ho! Good morning class! Good morning, Miss Zandile. And what was all that noise I was hearing down the passage? Poor Miss Bongi could hardly teach her Standard Twos. She teaches Nature Study, you know, she's very clever. But do you know what happens to naughty children? The white car will come for you and you won't even know it's coming. It's going to be standing there and it will be too late to run. Nobody can hear you scream because its engine makes such a loud noise. They're going to take out your eyes and take you to a far away place and nobody's going to see you ever again. (*She pauses as if she is listening to something*) And what is that I'm hearing . . . is that the white car? Ho ho ho ho! No, you are lucky this time. But I'm going to send you straight to the principal's office and he is going to give you this (*she demonstrates a hiding with her stick*).

Don't you know what day it is today? It is the 21st of September 1966 and the inspector is coming here today. You know the inspector does not understand our language (*she starts giggling*) and we don't want to embarrass him. (*Puts her hand over her mouth and laughs*) He cannot say our real names so we must all use white names in class today. Hands up those of you who don't have white names. We'll just have to give them to you. Wena you can be Violet. (*She points to different sections of the audience each time she mentions a different flower*) Petunia. Daisy. Sunflower and Innocentia . . . I don't know what that means . . . Do you know what name the inspector gave me in class today? Elsie. And I don't even look like an Elsie! Don't laugh! At least you are flowers. And do you know what he called Bongi? Moses! He couldn't even tell that she is a girl.

Lucy

The Lion, the Witch and the Wardrobe
C.S. Lewis
Dramatised by Adrian Mitchell

First performed in 1998 at the Royal Shakespeare Theatre, Stratford-upon-Avon and transferred to the Barbican Theatre, London in 1999.

This is the story of four children, LUCY (the youngest), Susan, Edmund and Peter, who are evacuated to the country during the London Blitz. Exploring the attic in their new home, LUCY discovers an old wardrobe – it is the gateway opening out into the Land of Narnia. Narnia is under the spell of the wicked White Witch and the four children find themselves caught up in an adventure leading up to a final struggle between the powers of good and evil.

In this scene, LUCY takes the other three children to meet her new friend, the faun Mr Tumnus. On arriving at his cave she finds that it has been ransacked and there is a notice saying that Mr Tumnus has been captured and is about to stand trial on the charge of 'comforting Her Majesty's enemies and fraternising with Humans'!

Published by Oberon Books, London

LUCY

We'll see Mr Tumnus first. He's the faun I told you about. Come on, then. This way. I'll go in first! Oh! (*The door has been wrenched off its hinges*) Mr Tumnus! (LUCY *plunges into the cave*) (*Off*) Oh no! Mr Tumnus! . . . (LUCY *emerges slowly, sadly carrying a wrecked painting*) Poor Mr Tumnus. It was a lovely cave . . . It's as if somebody dropped a bomb. Everything's broken – all the plates and cups. And this painting of Mr Tumnus' father – it's been slashed to pieces by somebody's claws. (*She throws it back into the cave*) . . . I found this notice pinned up. (*Reads from paper*) 'The former occupant of these premises, the Faun Tumnus, is under arrest and awaiting his trial on a charge of High Treason against her Imperial Majesty Jadis, Queen of Narnia, Chatelaine of Cair Paravel etcetcetc, also of comforting her said Majesty's enemies and fraternising with Humans. Signed MAUGRIM, Captain of the Secret Police. LONG LIVE THE QUEEN!' . . . She's not a real queen. She's the White Witch. All the wood people hate her. She cast a spell over the whole country so that it's always winter here. Always winter but never Christmas . . . That poor faun's in trouble because of me. He hid me from the Witch and showed me the way home. That's what is meant by comforting the Queen's enemies and fraternising with Humans. We've got to rescue him! . . . Look! A robin! It's the first bird I've seen here. I wonder if birds can talk in Narnia? (*Addressing the robin*) Please can you tell us where Tumnus the Faun has been taken? (LUCY *takes one step towards the bird, who flies to the next tree*) He wants us to follow him.

Snow-White

The Magic Mirror
A Fairy Play for Children
E.C. Brereton

This is a short play written especially for children to perform, and is the story of Snow-White and the Seven Dwarfs.

The Queen of Paflagonia has always been the fairest lady in the land, but now her magic mirror tells her that her step-daughter, the Princess Snow-White is fairer than she. The Queen immediately sends for her Huntsman to lure SNOW-WHITE into the forest and kill her. He is reluctant to do this, and when SNOW-WHITE pleads for her life he tells her she must run away before the Queen sends somebody else to kill her.

In this scene SNOW-WHITE has arrived at the House of the Seven Dwarfs set deep in the forest. She knocks at the door and getting no reply, opens it and steps inside. There she sees a table laid for seven very small people.

Published by Samuel French, London

SNOW-WHITE

I've knocked and knocked and nobody will answer the door! I wonder if this really is an empty house? (*She sees the table*) No, it can't be; here's a table laid for one, two, three, four, five, six, seven people. What a tiny table! and what tiny plates and dishes! (*She holds one up*) It's like a dolls' dinner-set! This must be a children's house! Oh dear! I wish they'd come home! I'm so hungry! Is there anything to eat on the table? (*She looks round*) Yes, bread and butter and milk. Then I must have some now, and when the people of the house come home I'm sure they'll forgive me when I tell them I've been two days and nights wandering in the forest with nothing to eat but nuts and blackberries! (*She pours some water into a glass and holds it up*) I don't call this glass very clean! It's all sticky finger-marks outside! (*She drinks and makes a face*) And the water tastes of stale tea-leaves and lime-juice mixed. And just look at the plates. They're grimed. (*She eats and puts the plate down*) And the dust on the table! I can write my name on it with my finger! Oh dear! (*She yawns*) I'm dreadfully tired! I think I'll just sit down and wait till the people of the house come home – and then – I'll explain – to them (*more and more drowsily till she falls asleep in the chair*).

Duchess
(A little dog)

The Mystery of the Pie and the Patty-Pan

Beatrix Potter
Dramatised by Rona Laurie

DUCHESS, a little dog, receives an invitation from her friend, Ribby, a pussy-cat, to come and have tea with her. Ribby has baked a very special pie for her in a pie dish with a pink rim, but DUCHESS is suspicious about the pie's contents. She would much prefer to eat her own veal and ham pie, baked with a little patty-pan in the middle.

In this opening scene, DUCHESS has just been handed a letter by the postman.

(*Note* This scene provides a good opportunity for young actors to work with props and practise both reading and writing a letter on stage.)

Published by Puffin Books, London

DUCHESS

A letter for me? Thank you, Postman. (*She opens the letter and reads it*) 'Dear Duchess, will you come to tea with me today? Come in good time, my dear Duchess, and we will have something so very nice. I am baking it in a pie-dish – a pie-dish with a pink rim. You never tasted anything so good! And *you* shall eat it all! I will eat muffins, my dear Duchess!' (*Then she goes into her house and writes a reply. Writing and reading aloud*) 'My dear Ribby, I will come with much pleasure at a quarter past four. But it is very strange. *I* was just going to invite you to come here, to supper, my dear Ribby, to eat something *most delicious.* I will come very punctually, my dear Ribby.' (*She pauses to think for a moment and then adds*) 'I hope it isn't mouse?' That does not look quite polite. (*She scratches out 'isn't mouse'*) 'I hope it will be fine.' (*She goes to her front door, sees the postman passing her gate and gives him the letter*) Will you please deliver this to Mrs Ribston? (*She goes into her house and reads Ribby's letter again*) (*To herself*) I am dreadfully afraid it *will* be mouse! I really couldn't, *couldn't* eat mouse pie. And I shall have to eat it, because it is a party. And *my* pie was going to be veal and ham. A pink and white pie-dish! And so is mine; just like Ribby's dishes; they were both bought at Tabitha Twitchit's. (*She goes into her larder, takes the pie off a shelf and looks at it*) It is all ready to put into the oven. Such a lovely pie-crust; and I put in a little tin patty-pan to hold up the crust; and I made a hole in the middle with a fork to let out the steam – Oh I do wish I could eat my own pie, instead of a pie made of mouse! (*She goes to her table and reads Ribby's letter again*) 'A pink and white pie-dish – and *you* shall eat it *all*.' 'You' means me – then Ribby is not going to even taste the pie herself? A pink and white pie-dish! Ribby is sure to go out and buy muffins . . . Oh what a good idea! (*She jumps up, delighted with her own cleverness*) Why shouldn't I rush along and put my pie into Ribby's oven when Ribby isn't there?

Tabitha
(A mother cat)

Tom Kitten and His Friends

Based on a story by Beatrix Potter
Play by Adrian Mitchell

First performed at the Unicorn Theatre for Children in 1995, *The Tale of Tom Kitten* is one of four adaptations of stories under the main title.

A mother cat – TABITHA – is expecting her friends to tea and is determined that her three kittens, Mittens, Moppet and Tom will look their very best.

In this scene she comes out of her house to call them in from the garden.

Published by Samuel French, London

TABITHA

Stop playing, Kittens! Tom and Mittens! Stop it, Moppet! . . . I am expecting friends to tea. So come indoors immediately. I must dress you before the fine company arrives. (*TABITHA chases the kittens indoors*) . . . So my visitors say: What fine kittens you are: (*She sings – combing Tom*)

> Take a spiky little comb
> To your whiskers and your tail . . .

(*Tom scratches TABITHA. Shocked, she licks her paw*) Tom Kitten you should be ashamed of yourself. Come, Moppet and Mittens – put on your clean pinafores and tuckers . . . Now Thomas, I have all sorts of elegant clothes to dress you up in. (*Pushing him into his suit*) You shall wear your sky-blue suit. Hold out your arms. Breathe in, Thomas. Oh dear. There goes a button . . . There! You're done. Now all three of you are beautiful. But I want you all to be out of my way while I make hot buttered toast. Out you go, into the garden! (*She pushes them out*) Now keep your frocks clean, children! You must walk on your hind legs. Keep away from the dirty ash-pit, and from Sally Henny Penny and from the pigsty. And don't have anything to do with the Puddle-Ducks. (*She goes back into her kitchen and busies herself making toast*) (*She sings*)

> We have a little garden
> A garden of our own
> And every day we water there
> The seeds that we have sown.

(*TABITHA looks out of the door*) Mittens! Moppet! Tom Kitten! Whatever do you think you're doing – sitting on the garden wall with no clothes on? (*She pulls them off the wall and cuffs them and drives them back indoors*) There'll be no hot buttered toast for you. My friends will arrive for tea in a minute, and you are not fit to be seen. I am affronted. Yes, I am affronted. (*The kittens are shooed out of sight*) What have I done to deserve such kittens? Still, the garden's looking at its best for my visitors. (*The church clock chimes four*) Four o'clock. Tea-time. And here come my friends. (*Her three friends come into the garden*) There's hot buttered toast for everyone. (*She brings out a tray piled high with toast and tea*) My children are all upstairs in bed. They are unwell. They have measles. In fact they're totally covered in spots. Yes, absolutely, under their fur. Do sit down, friends. It doesn't do to keep hot buttered toast a-waiting.

Whizziwig
(An alien)

Whizziwig

Malorie Blackman

Published in 1995, *Whizziwig* is now a children's serial on Carlton Television.

WHIZZIWIG is a small, friendly alien whose space-ship has just crash-landed on Ben's roof. She is described as more 'girl' than 'boy' – but then they don't have girls or boys on their planet. Ben has complained to his Mum and Dad that a small furry thing is bouncing about in his bedroom, but they tell him to lie down and go to sleep. The bouncing continues.

In this scene WHIZZIWIG appears for the first time on top of Ben's wardrobe and insists on introducing herself.

Published by Puffin Books, London

WHIZZIWIG

My name is Whizziwig. I am sorry if I frightened you. I did not mean to. I would have spoken to you before, but it has taken me this long to learn all the spoken languages on this planet . . . I'm on top of the wardrobe. Can I come down now? (*WHIZZIWIG bounces down from the wardrobe and bounces towards Ben's bed*) I am an Oricon. What the people on your world would call a wish-giver . . . I was passing your planet four days ago on the way to visit my auntie, when some space debris hit my ship and I had to make an emergency landing on your roof . . . It is still up on your roof. It will have to stay there until I can fix it. (*WHIZZIWIG sighs*) I have been bouncing around this immediate area ever since I arrived and I have yet to fix a single thing . . . It will take wishes to fix my ship. And I can only fix it by giving people whatever they wish for . . . I can't give you a new bike. (*WHIZZIWIG rocks to the left and then to the right*) Nope . . . I can only grant wishes if you make a wish for someone else . . . You have to wish almost without realising what you're doing – it has to be unselfish wishing . . . That's the way it works . . . I am an accidental wish-maker . . . There are different types of Oricons. Some make dreams come true, others make daydreams come true, some give you exactly what you want, some give you the exact opposite of what you want. I grant wishes – but only to those who make wishes for someone else . . . that is my job. It is tough, but someone has to do it!

Fairy

The Wild Swans

Hans Christian Andersen
Adapted by Rona Laurie

This is the story of Eleven Princes who are turned into wild swans by their wicked stepmother, and their sister, the Princess Elise, who runs away into the forest in search of them.

In the forest Elise meets an Old Woman who gives her some berries and tells her where the wild swans are living.

In this scene Elise has found her eleven 'swan' brothers, and lies down to sleep with the youngest swan's head resting in her lap. In a dream a FAIRY appears to her with stinging nettles in her hand, and tells Elise what she must do to save the Princes – weave eleven long-sleeved shirts from stinging nettles, despite the pain of picking them, and throw one over each swan. All this must be done in complete silence; one word from Elise, and her brothers' lives will be forfeit.

FAIRY

Do you remember the old woman who gave you berries in the forest? I was that old woman, in disguise. I have come to tell you how you can free your brothers from the Queen's wicked spell. But it will not be easy. Have you courage and patience enough? Your tender fingers will feel burning pain and your heart will be tormented with grief. Do you see these stinging nettles in my hand? They grow around this place where you are sleeping. But only those which grow here or on the graves in churchyards are of any use. Remember that. You must pluck them though they sting your hand. (*The FAIRY touches Elise's hand with a nettle*) You must trample them with your feet and get yarn from them and with this yarn you must weave eleven shirts with long sleeves. When they are all made, throw them over the eleven wild swans and the spell will be broken. They will become human again. But remember this, Elise, from the moment you begin your work until it is finished you must not speak a word. If you do, the first word that you speak will plunge like a dagger into the hearts of your brothers. Their life depends on your silence. Remember this! (*She drops a nettle by Elise's hand and exits*)

Mikey
(A baby dragon)

Beauty and the Beast
Nicholas Stuart Gray

This is the story of a bad-tempered Prince, who is sent to live in an empty castle by the absent-minded Wizard Hodge. Forgotten for five hundred years he has become a beast, but is eventually tamed by the Merchant's daughter, Beauty.

In this scene Beauty has gone home to see her family, having promised to return in a week. Now the week is up. Beauty has failed to return and the Beast is in a terrible rage. The table is set for supper but the Beast is unable to eat anything. MIKEY, the Wizard's nephew tries to comfort him. He is the Beast's only companion – a small dragon who has only just sprouted wings and is afraid of flying. He tries to persuade the Beast to eat something. MIKEY himself is very hungry.

Published by Samuel French, London

MIKEY

Isn't she here? . . . It's after ten . . . The bell has started to strike four times, now, and each time you've stopped it . . . It's long after ten. She isn't coming . . . I'm hungry . . . Could I have something to eat? I've washed my hands three times . . . and the food has all been heated up twice, and I'm simply starving. (*Pause*) I've brushed my wings . . . I brushed my wings twice, and I put a jug of roses in Beauty's room. Do you think she'll be pleased? That is, if she ever comes back . . . Wouldn't you like some food? I'm awfully hungry . . . (*The beast rises and goes swiftly to the table where he lifts the roses and dashes them to the ground. He sweeps the table clear with his paws –* MIKEY *watches awestruck*) You have made an awful mess. (*He picks up a roasted chicken-leg, and is about to eat it when he sees the Beast reeling*) Beast! What's the matter with you? (MIKEY *goes to him*) Don't cry. Please don't cry. I don't know what to do. I didn't know you could cry. (*He wipes his own eyes and nibbles the chicken*) I'm frightened. Where's Beauty? She ought to be here. She could make him listen. Beast . . . Beast . . . don't cry like that. You'll die. Oh, dear, I wish Uncle were here. (*He looks out of the window. He is still eating the chicken desperately. Calling*) Uncle! Oh, he can't hear. I don't know any magic to bring him here. (*The Beast moans. He is going to die*) What shall I do? What can I do? I've forgotten the only magic I ever knew. Uncle taught me a spell. It would have brought him here like lightning . . . but I can't remember. Dear Beast, don't die! (*The Beast moans and opens his eyes*) Oh, Beast, are you all right? Do be all right . . . (MIKEY *sobs*) Oooooooh . . . (*He sucks the chicken bone and looks at it helplessly*) I might make up a spell. But it wouldn't work for me. I'm not a magician or anything. (*He sniffs and holds up the bone*)

> All the magic I have known
> Please be in this chicken bone . . .
> Magic, magic, magic dear,
> Oh, do bring my uncle here.

It won't of course. (*But the Wizard is standing in the window*) Uncle Hodge! Oh, Uncle Hodge! (*Frantic with relief*) That was me. Uncle . . . the Beast let Beauty go home for a week, and she hasn't come back . . . and he's dying, Uncle. Can we send a message? (*The Wizard shakes his head*) I . . . I . . . I could tell her . . .that he needs her . . . You told me where she lives . . . (MIKEY *jumps up on the window seat and looks down. He recoils from the height*) . . . I must fly . . . I've got to fly . . . (*He jumps from the window*)

Loll
(Gloucestershire)

Cider with Rosie

Laurie Lee

A Stage Adaptation by James Roose-Evans

Performed at the Hampstead Theatre in 1963 and later transferred to the Garrick Theatre, London. The poet, Laurie Lee, remembers scenes from his childhood in a Cotswold village.

In this scene, Laurie Lee, known as LOLL to his family and friends, is sitting in school waiting for the arrival of the new Headmistress, Miss Wardle. As she enters, he sniffs and is immediately told to go outside and give his nose a good blow.

Published by Samuel French, London

LOLL

(*LOLL sniffs . . . he leaves the classroom area and sits on the very edge of the stage*) Of course I don't really belong to that lot at all. I'm summat different to them. I'm a – I'm a – young king. Yes! Placed secretly here in order to mix with the commoners. (*He sniffs*) There is clearly a mystery about my birth. One day the secret will be told. One day, they'll see, a gold coach with footmen in uniform will turn up suddenly, just like that! outside our kitchen door, and our Mother will cry and they'll stand very solemn and respectful to our Marge and Doth and Phyll and Jack and Tone, and then I shall drive off to my palace. I shall eat bacon and eggs off my throne. Course I shall be generous. I won't throw my brothers in a dungeon. No. Instead I shall give them a banquet of cakes and jellies and – things! And all my sisters, our Marge, our Doth, our Phyll, they shall have princes and they shall live in a palace in . . . (*His imagination runs out here*) Where shall it be? Ah yes. Stroud! . . . (*The children in the classroom rise swiftly and start singing the national anthem, conducted by Miss Wardley*)

[**Chorus** (*singing*) God save our gracious King . . .]

. . . And when I am King, Miss Wardley shall curtsy!

(*He joins the rest in place, singing loudly, aggressively*)

[**Chorus** (*singing*) Long to reign over us, God save our King!]

(*All sit*)

Billy

The Giraffe and the Pelly and Me

Roald Dahl

A play with music for children, adapted by Vicky Ireland

Commissioned by Polka Theatre for Children, Wimbledon, London and performed by them in 1992.

BILLY longs to see 'The Grubber' – a deserted sweet-shop near his house – returned to its former glory. His dream seems impossible until he meets a strange trio of animals, the Giraffe, the Pelly and the Monkey, also known as 'The Ladderless Window-Cleaning Company'.

In this opening scene, BILLY introduces the audience to 'The Grubber' and we meet the Giraffe for the first time.

Published by Samuel French, London

BILLY

Hallo. My name's Billy. Not far from where I live, there's something very strange. It's a house. Not an ordinary house, but a strange old one made of wood. It stands by itself on the side of the road. (*The lights go up on The Grubber at back of the stage – a sign on the window reads 'For Sail'*) Look, there it is. (*He walks carefully up to the house and reads the sign on the window*) 'For Sail' . . . Hmmmm. It's been like this for ages, all empty and shut up. Wish I could get in and explore, but the door's always locked . . . (*Looking through the window*) It's all dark and dusty inside, but I know the ground floor used to be a shop, because look, you can still just read the lettering up there, it's a bit faded, over the window . . .'The Grubber' . . . ? (*Mum enters*) Mum . . .? What does the word 'Grubber' mean, do you know – the word that's over the shop? . . . A sweet-shop! . . . Wow! So that's what it was. It must have been a lovely old sweet-shop. Oh, I wish I could buy it . . . then I'd make it into a grubber all over again. I'd do anything to have my own sweet-shop. Just think, Mum, what it would be like . . . Caramel Fudge – that'd be grand . . . Sugar Pig Snorters . . . Butter Gumballs? . . . (*To audience*) But the next time I went to visit 'The Grubber', something had happened – something exciting . . . somebody had scraped off the 'For Sail' sign, and painted instead – look – 'Soled'. Soled! I was too late. Now that old sweet-shop would never be mine . . .The next day I was back. Hey, look at the door, it's changed, it's fantastic. Hang on, no-one could use a door like that except a giant. (*Reading the window sign*) 'The L-ladder-less Window Cleaning Company . . . Get Your Windows Cleaned Without a Lot of Dirty Ladders Leaning Against Your House.' What on earth's it all about! (*One of the windows on the top floor begins to open outwards*) Just a minute, something's happening. Oh crumbs! (*The Giraffe's head appears at the window*) Wow!

Hansel

Hansel and Gretel

An adaptation from *Grimm's Fairy Tales*
Jean Marlow

Grimm's Fairy Tales were written by the Brothers Grimm in 1812 and were collected from German folk tales, popular stories of that time and ancient manuscripts.

HANSEL and his little sister Gretel, live with their father and cruel stepmother in a small cottage on the edge of the forest. Food is very scarce and the family are almost starving. Their stepmother has always disliked the children and persuades their father to take them deep into the forest and leave them there. That evening he sets off with the children on the pretence of collecting wood. He gives HANSEL a crust of bread tied up in a red-spotted handkerchief. HANSEL is suspicious and as they walk further into the forest he breaks up the crust of bread, leaving a trail of crumbs behind them. When they reach the deepest part of the forest, their father tells them he must leave them for a while but will be back to fetch them later.

In this scene the children are becoming anxious. It is nearly an hour since their father left them and Gretel is starting to cry.

HANSEL

Don't cry Gretel. Father didn't mean to leave us all alone in the forest. I know he didn't . . . please don't cry! (*He takes a red-spotted handkerchief from his pocket and shakes it out*) See. I've broken up the crust of bread he gave us and left a trail of crumbs leading all the way back home again. Think how happy he'll be when he finds us all tucked up and snug in our beds tomorrow morning. (*He laughs*) Look! The moon is coming up from behind the clouds and we can easily find our way back. See – there are the breadcrumbs. They start from here and they go all along the path and . . . Oh no! the trail has stopped . . . Of course, the birds have eaten them up! There's only little bits left. And I simply can't remember the way back . . . Never mind, father will come and find us very soon . . . Don't worry, I'll look after you . . . How beautiful everything looks in the moonlight . . . And over there I can see a little house. I wonder if there's anyone at home. Come on. Let's go and see. (*They hurry towards the house and then stop and sniff*) Mmm! What a lovely smell! Like the gingerbread mother used to bake! (*They move in closer*) It *is* gingerbread! It's covered in gingerbread! And look! The stones around the door are little cakes! (*He goes up to the front door and raises the door knocker*) Chocolate! The door knocker's made of chocolate. (*He breaks off a piece and starts to eat it – then frightened, he jumps back*) What's that? I thought I heard something . . . No, it's only the wind. (*He creeps up to the door again*) Look, Gretel. The windows – they're made of barley sugar. (*He breaks off a piece of windowpane and hands another piece to Gretel. The front door opens suddenly and an old lady pokes out her head at them*) Oh! . . . I'm sorry! I didn't mean to break your window. But we were so hungry . . . we haven't eaten all day . . . I'll buy you a new door knocker . . . And my father will put in a new pane of er– barley sugar for you . . . Please forgive us!

Pascal
(Played in the film by a 5-year-old boy)

The Red Balloon

Anthony Clark

Adapted for the stage from a film by Albert Lamorisse

First performed by the Contact Theatre, Manchester and then by the Royal National Theatre in 1996. It is set in Paris in 1956 and tells the story of PASCAL, a lonely little boy who is bored at home and tormented at school, until he makes friends with a big red balloon.

PASCAL's classmates have snatched his satchel, broken his new pen and torn up his homework book, then run off leaving him all alone in the pouring rain. He sees a kitten crying in the street and unable to find out who it belongs to, takes it home with him. He names it 'Hercule'.

Next morning PASCAL's mother insists that he takes 'Hercule' back to where he found him. PASCAL sulkily collects a cardboard box and lifts the kitten into it. His mother asks to see his homework and in this scene he tries to explain what has happend to it. He leaves the house with 'Hercule' in the box. On his way down the street he meets his friend 'Raggedy' the Tramp. 'Raggedy' likes cats and PASCAL persuades him to take care of 'Hercule'.

Published by Oberon Books, London

PASCAL

It was an accident. It was raining, and I was running to get home, and I dropped my book, and it fell open, and the page with my homework on fell in a puddle, and all the ink ran, and then I tore out the page because I didn't want to ruin the whole book . . . I promise you, it's true . . . And I dropped my pen . . . And the nib broke . . . I couldn't help it Maman. Everything fell out of my satchel. I had to protect Hercule from the rain. Cats don't like water do they? I had to put him in my satchel, and then I wanted to keep my books dry, so I put them under my jersey. But they wouldn't stay and they kept falling out . . . (*PASCAL puts Hercule into the box*) Come on Hercule, or we'll be late. Say goodbye . . . Hercule say 'thank you'. Maiow! . . . (*He leaves*)

(*The street. A Tramp is asleep beside an old dustbin. The Tramp stirs. Enter PASCAL with Hercule still in the cardboard box*) You don't remember him, do you? Do you remember me? . . .Yesterday, . . . He was crying in the rain. Cats don't like the rain . . . I'm not allowed to keep Hercule, because I live in a flat. And Maman and Papa don't like cats, though they pretend they do. Papa says he'll ask the concierge, if I can keep Hercule, but he'll forget. He always does. And Maman said its not fair. Can you look after him for me? He's never a nuisance. He likes playing all the time. I'll bring you my scraps for him to eat. He doesn't eat much, he's got a very small stomach. Please? Just until Mama and Papa stop arguing, and Papa stops worrying about money, and he remembers to ask the concierge to change the rules . . . Don't lose him, will you? . . . Be careful . . . See you soon Hercule. Raggedy, will look after you.

Kay

The Snow Queen

Hans Christian Andersen
Adapted by Jean Marlow

There was once a wicked goblin who invented a magic mirror so powerful that whatever was reflected in it appeared hideous and distorted. All the other goblins thought it a huge joke and planned to fly it up to heaven and make fun of the angels there. But as soon as they got near to heaven the mirror began to shake so much that they had to let go of it and it came crashing down to earth and shattered into millions and millions of pieces. These tiny splinters of glass went flying all over the world. Some of them flew into people's eyes, so that whatever they looked at appeared hateful to them. Other splinters pierced their chests, turning their hearts into blocks of ice.

Two children, KAY and Gerda, lived next door to each other high in the rooftops of a small Scandinavian town. They were the best of friends. KAY would often spend the afternoon with Gerda and together they'd listen to her grandmother telling them fairy stories. KAY's favourite story was always the one about the snow queen.

In this scene it is winter and as KAY looks out of the window, the snow is beginning to fall.

KAY

(*Looking out of the window*) Gerda! Come and see! It's starting to snow again. Look at the snowflakes – how beautiful they are. Each one is different. (*He holds his arm out of the window to catch a flake on the sleeve of his jacket*) See – this one is like a marvellous flower, or a star – a ten-pointed star. They're much more beautiful than real flowers. It's snowing faster now – the flakes are getting really big! They're whirling about and swarming like white bees. Do you suppose they have a queen like real bees? Your grandma says they do. She says that when the snowflakes start to swarm, the queen is always there – the Snow Queen. (*Leaning out of the window*) Oh how I wish I could see her. I don't believe she is a real queen at all. I'd like to catch her. Then I'd make her sit on the hot stove and watch her melt! (*He laughs – then suddenly turns from the window*) Oh! – I've got something in my eye. (*He rubs his eye*) And there's a pain deep in my heart. Like a needle stabbing me. (*Gerda goes to put her arm around him*) It's alright – it's gone now. It doesn't hurt any more . . . (*He pushes her away*) Why are you crying? What a stupid ugly girl you are. And you look even uglier when you cry. And your voice – it's horrible – like that old crow that sits up on the roof. 'Caw, caw.' (*He imitates Gerda's voice*) 'Oh poor Kay. Where does it hurt? Caw! Caw! Caw!' (*He takes up a stick*) And I hate these flowers in their stupid pots. I'm going to knock their heads off. (*He hits out at the flowers. Gerda tries to stop him*) Leave me alone! Or I'll knock your head off too! (*He runs over to the window and looks down into the street*) The snow is getting deeper. I'm going out to play. No you can't come with me. I'm going to take my new sledge. And I'm going to go tobogganing with the other children in the square!

Mole
(Any age)

Toad of Toad Hall

A Play from Kenneth Grahame's Book *The Wind in the Willows*
A.A. Milne

First produced at the Liverpool Playhouse in 1929, it is based around the adventures of the foolish Toad and his friends: the kindly Rat, the wise Badger and the gentle, but very nervous, MOLE.

This scene takes place at night in the middle of the Wild Wood – a frightening place in the moonlight – with the snow thick on the ground. MOLE comes limping in through the trees, looking over his shoulder as he hears the mocking laughter of the creatures who inhabit the wood. His friends had warned him not to come here and now he is hopelessly lost.

Published by Samuel French, London

MOLE

(*Hopefully*) Ratty! (*In sudden panic as a bat crosses the stage*) What's that? Pooh! It's nothing! *I'm* not frightened! . . . I do wish Ratty was here. He's so comforting, is Ratty. Or the brave Mr Toad. *He'd* frighten them all away. (*He seems to hear the sound of mocking laughter*) What's that? (*He looks round anxiously*) Ratty always said, 'Don't go into the Wild Wood.' That's what he always said. 'Not by yourself,' he said. 'It isn't safe,' he said. 'We *never* do,' he said. That's what Ratty said. But I thought I knew better. There he was, dear old Rat, dozing in front of the fire, and I thought if I just slipped out, just to see what the Wild Wood was like – what's that – ? (*He breaks off suddenly and turns up stage, fearing an attack from behind. There is nothing*) I should be safer up against a tree. Why didn't I think of that before? (*He settles himself at the foot of a tree*) Ratty would have thought of it, he's so wise. Oh, Ratty, I wish you were here! It's so much more friendly with two! (*His head droops on his chest*) . . . (*waking up suddenly*) What's that? . . . (*frightened*) Who is it? . . . (*Rat enters and crosses to Mole. He has a lantern in his hand and a cudgel over his shoulder.* MOLE *is crawling around distraught, almost in tears*) Oh, Rat! . . . Oh, Ratty, I've been so frightened, you can't think . . . (*sitting*) Oh, Ratty. I don't know how to tell you, but I'm afraid you'll never want me for a companion again, but I can't, I simply *can't* go all that way back home now . . . I'm aching all over. Oh, Ratty, do forgive me. I feel as if I must just sit here for ever and ever and ever, and I'm not a bit frightened now you're with me – and – and I think I want to go to sleep.

Boy

The Witches

Roald Dahl

Adapted by David Wood

First performed at the Lyceum Theatre, Sheffield in 1992 and then at the Duke of York's Theatre, London.

BOY and his grandmother are staying at The Hotel Magnificent, where the Witches are holding their annual meeting, supposedly of The Royal Society of the Prevention of Cruelty to Children. It is presided over by the Grand High Witch, who is planning to 'rub out' every child in England with her latest formula, which will turn them all into mice. This potion is to be injected into tasty sweets and chocs. A greedy boy, Bruno Jenkins is also staying with his parents at the hotel and becomes her first victim. BOY, who has been searching for his missing pet mice, William and Mary, has wandered into the ballroom where the meeting is being held and quickly hides behind a screen. But the Witches smell him out and force him to drink the rest of the potion.

In this scene, BOY comes scampering back into the ballroom as a 'mouse'. He sniffs around, calling for Bruno. He meets Bruno, now also a 'mouse', eating a chunk of bread. At first Bruno refuses to believe what has happened to him and then begins to cry. BOY tries to explain the advantages of being a mouse and then plans their escape.

Published by Samuel French, London

BOY

(*Calling*) Bruno! Bruno Jenkins! (*No reply.* BOY *frisks around happily. To the audience*) I should be sad. I should feel desperate. I mean, I've never dreamed of being a mouse, like I've dreamed of being, say, a film star. But now that I *am* one, I'm beginning to see the advantages. I know mice sometimes get poisoned or caught in traps but boys sometimes get killed too – run over or get some awful illness. Boys have to go to school. Mice don't. Mice don't have to pass exams. When mice grow up they don't have to go out to work. Mm. It's no bad thing to be a mouse. I'm as free as William and Mary. Hope they're all right. (*Bruno, dressed as a mouse, enters eating a chunk of bread – to Bruno*) Hallo, Bruno. (*Bruno nods*) What have you found? . . . An ancient fish paste sandwich. Pretty good. Bit pongy . . . Listen, Bruno. Now we're both mice, I think we ought to start thinking about the future . . . (*Bruno stops eating*) But you're a mouse too, Bruno . . . Look at your paws . . . Don't be silly, Bruno. There are worse things than being a mouse. You can live in a hole . . . And you can creep into the larder at night and nibble through all the packets of biscuits and cornflakes and stuff. You can stuff yourself silly . . . Maybe your rich father will get you a special little mouse-fridge all to yourself. One you can open . . . We'll go and see my grandmother. She'll understand. She knows all about witches . . . The witches who turned us into mice. The Grand High Witch gave you a chocolate, remember? . . . Follow me to Grandmother's room. Down the corridor, run like mad . . . No talking. And don't let anyone see you. Don't forget that anyone who catches you will try to kill you! . . . Come on.

Arrietty

The Borrowers

Mary Norton

First published in 1952, and made into a BBC Television series adapted by Richard Carpenter in 1992.

Beneath the floor behind the kitchen clock live a family of tiny people; Pod and his wife, Homily, and their young daughter ARRIETTY. Everything they have, clothes, furniture, food and even their own names, are borrowed from the human 'beans' upstairs, and they call themselves 'The Borrowers'.

Pod has been seen as he was climbing down the curtains, by a human 'Boy', while he was on his last borrowing expedition. The time has come to warn ARRIETTY about human 'beans' and how dangerous it is to venture upstairs alone. Over supper, Pod and Homily tell her how her cousin Eggletina – who had never been told about the dangers of 'Upstairs' – had climbed up there on her own and never been seen again. Her father, Uncle Hendreary, was broken-hearted, and he and his family emigrated very soon after-wards. It was thought that the cat had got Eggletina.

Published by Puffin Books, London

ARRIETTY

Why did you tell me this? Now? Tonight? . . . You think they'll get a cat? (*She sets down her cup of soup*) Couldn't we emigrate? . . . Supposing that *I* went out, like Eggletina did, and the cat ate *me*. Then you and papa would emigrate. Wouldn't you? (*Her voice falters*) Wouldn't you? (*Her eyes fill with tears*) I was only thinking that I'd like to be there – to emigrate too. Uneaten . . . It's not that I'm afraid. (*Angrily*) I like cats. I bet the cat didn't eat Eggletina. I bet she just ran away because she hated being cooped up . . . day after day . . . week after week . . . year after year . . . Like I do! (*A sob*) . . . Oh, I know papa is a wonderful Borrower. I know we've managed to stay when all the others have gone. But what has it done for us, in the end? I don't think it's so clever to live on alone, for ever and ever, in a great, big, half-empty house, under the floor, with no one to talk to, no one to play with, nothing to see but dust and passages, no light but candlelight and firelight and what comes through the cracks. Eggletina had brothers and Eggletina had half-brothers; Eggletina had a tame mouse; Eggletina had yellow boots with jet buttons and Eggletina did get out – just once!

Maria Jones
(Aged 10 or 11)

The Box of Delights

John Masefield

A mysterious Punch and Judy man gives Kay Harker the magic Box of Delights, which takes him back into the days of King Arthur and beyond that to Troy. Abner Brown's gang are trying to find the magic box and they kidnap Kay's friend, little MARIA JONES.

In this scene the gang have released MARIA after questioning, and here she describes her ordeal to Kay.

Published by Heinemann Educational Books, Oxford

MARIA

I don't know where I've been. I've been scrobbled just like a green-horn. I knew what it would be, not taking a pistol. Well I pity them if ever I get near them again. They won't scrobble Maria Jones a second time . . . I was no sooner in the room than a great iron door shot up behind me and there I was, shut in. Then rather high up on the wall an iron shutter slid to one side and there was an iron grille with what I took to be a lady's face; and a very silky female voice said, 'Miss Maria Jones, please forgive any inconvenience we may have caused you in bringing you here and, above all, don't be afraid.' 'I'm not used to being afraid,' I said; but all the same I was afraid. 'We only brought you here,' the female said, 'because we hope that you may be interested. We are rather in need of a dashing young associate at the moment and we wondered whether we might persuade you to become that.' 'Oh,' I said, 'what are you: a gang of crooks?' 'Oh no,' she said, 'a business community.' 'Oh,' I said, 'what business does your community do?' . . . 'You would soon learn if you would join us.' 'Why do you want me?' I asked. 'Well, you are young,' she said, 'and full of dash. It's an interesting world for our younger agents; lots of motor cars, lots of aeroplanes. Life is one long, gay social whirl.' 'And what is the work?' I asked. 'Ah,' she said, 'we shall discuss that if you expressed a willingness to become one of us.' 'If your job was honest,' I said, 'you'd say what it is. It can't be very nice, or it wouldn't have you in it.' 'If children are pert here,' she said, 'we make them into dog-biscuit. Many a good watch-dog is barking now on insolent little chits like you.' So I said, 'If ladies are pert to me I make them into cat's-meat. Many a good caterwaul have I fed on meat like you, cold.'

Violet Beauregarde
(American)

Charlie and the Chocolate Factory
Roald Dahl
Adapted by Richard R. George

First presented in 1973 by Richard George and the VI Grade Class of Charlotte Elementary School, New York.

Mr Willy Wonka has just re-opened his Chocolate Factory and announces in the newspapers that he has hidden five golden tickets in five Wonka Candy Bars. These could be found anywhere, in any shop, any town and in any country in the world. Whoever finds one of these tickets will have a special tour of Mr Wonka's new factory and take home enough chocolate to last them the rest of their lives. In this scene, four golden tickets have been found. The Narrator is on stage announcing the winners and inviting them to say a few words to the audience. One of these winners is VIOLET BEAUREGARDE.

Published by Puffin Books, London

VIOLET BEAUREGARDE

(*Chewing ferociously on gum, waving arms excitedly, talking in a rapid and loud manner, from somewhere in audience*) I'm a gum-chewer normally, but when I heard about these ticket things of Mr Wonka's, I laid off the gum and switched to candy bars in the hope of striking it lucky. *Now*, of course, I'm right back on gum. I just *adore* gum. I can't do without it. I munch it all day long except for a few minutes at mealtimes when I take it out and stick it behind my ear for safe-keeping. To tell you the honest truth, I simply wouldn't feel *comfortable* if I didn't have that little wedge of gum to chew on every moment of the day, I really wouldn't. My mother says it's not ladylike and it looks ugly to see a girl's jaws going up and down like mine do all the time, but I don't agree. And who's she to criticise, anyway, because if you ask me, I'd say that *her* jaws are going up and down almost as much as mine are just from *yelling* at me every minute of the day. And now, it may interest you to know that this piece of gum I'm chewing right at this moment is one I've been working on for over *three months solid*. That's a record, that is. It's beaten the record held by my best friend, Miss Cornelia Prinzmetel. And was she ever mad! It's my most treasured possession now, this piece of gum is. At nights, I just stick it on the end of the bedpost, and it's as good as ever in the mornings . . .

Perduta

Daughters of Venice
Don Taylor

First produced by the Chiswick Youth Theatre at the Waterman's Arts Centre in 1991, and then professionally by the Quercus Theatre Company at the Wilde Theatre in 1993. Set in eighteenth century Venice, the 'Daughters' of the title are the orphans taken in and cared for by the sisters of the Convent of the Pieta – famous for its choir and orchestra, the 'Coro'.

It is Carnival time and PERDUTA, who works with the Coro as a copyist, is sitting in the library sorting music with four other young girls. They are bored and complaining that nothing ever happens to them, when two young Italians, Pazzo and Grimaldo enter disguised, not very convincingly, as nuns.

A composite speech from Act II. Published by Samuel French, London

PERDUTA

Good-evening, Sisters . . . (*To Pazzo*) I don't think I know you, Sister.
Who are you? . . . (*To the other girls*) Leave it to me. I've got an idea
. . . Sisters? . . . Do you know what happened last week, Sisters? . .
. Two men got in here. Actually into the convent! Terribly not
allowed! . . . It was thrillingly exciting! . . . Do you know what happened? . . . They got torn to pieces. Both of them. The bits were
thrown into the canal. (*The men laugh*) No, really, I'm serious! Just
up that corridor, there are a thousand girls of all ages. They've only
just got off to sleep. They're really tough girls, they are, from the
streets of Venice, all ages, up to nineteen . . . They get very angry,
those girls do, if the convent is desecrated. They fell on those two
poor fellows like a pack of wolves. Didn't they girls? . . . You could-
n't help feeling sorry for them . . . They were simply overwhelmed!
. . . They were very brave and strong. But they didn't have a chance
. . . Not against a thousand girls in a raging fury! . . . Tore them to
pieces. It was terrible. We little ones had to clear up all the blood.
Then some of the brawny nuns, the tough ones with big muscles,
put all the bits in a basket and threw them into the canal. The
Doge's secret police came here a week later, looking for them.
Apparently they were criminals on the run. But they didn't find a
thing. Not one shred of flesh! Not a chip of bone! Not a fingernail!
Not a hair! They just disappeared. From the face of the earth. For
ever and ever. Amen . . . They got caught, of course. If they'd
managed to slip out without being suspected . . . (*The men run off*)
And next time you want to be a nun, make sure your boots aren't
showing!

Dinah

The Demon Headmaster
Gillian Cross

Something is very wrong indeed at DINAH's new school. The children are strangely neat and much too well behaved. She asks herself why is this, and why does she find herself conforming? Determined to find out the secret of the Headmaster's control and aided by her foster brothers, Lloyd and Harvey, she gradually unravels the mystery of the sinister Headmaster.

Young Harvey has found out that something very odd is going on at morning assembly. He and Lloyd are never allowed to join in with the other children but have to stay outside doing maths under the supervision of the Prefects. Next morning he excuses himself on the pretext of having to go to the toilet and creeps up to the Hall and looks in. The whole school are staring fixedly at the Headmaster and chanting in a regular monotone. When he asks DINAH about this she tells him that they have been watching a film, but he knows this is not true.

In this scene the two boys are questioning DINAH about what actually happens in assembly and gradually she begins to realise that she and the rest of the school are being hypnotised.

Published by Puffin Modern Classics, London

DINAH

That's it! The first day, when I went into Assembly, I didn't look at the Headmaster's eyes when the others did. I closed mine. And I heard him hypnotise everyone else. But then he caught me. I just had time to think *remember it, remember it* – and then I was hypnotised and I forgot. Until Harvey brought it back. *The Headmaster hypnotises everyone in Assembly* . . . It's a good way to keep everyone in order. And you know how he likes order. While they're hypnotised, he tells them what to do when they wake up. And they can't help doing it. Like me saying those things. And I think – I think he probably makes us learn things, parrot-fashion, while we're hypnotised. Then, when we're awake, we can remember them and write them down . . . We're not learning to *think*. We're just learning to repeat things. Like robots. It looks good, but it's no use at all . . . Some people can't be hypnotised. Has he ever tried it with you? Gazed into your eyes and told you you were tired? . . . He's cruel and terrifying, and he's got an obsession with tidiness, but he's not silly. He's very, very clever. He's got a whole school full of children who will do precisely what he wants. He must feel very powerful. Very powerful. If I were him, I don't think I'd be satisfied with having one measly school in my power! . . . Think of it. He's got a whole army of people – people like me – who'll do and say exactly what he wants. Why should he stop there? Sooner or later, he's going to 'want to do something with his army'.

Eva
(German – aged 9)

Kindertransport

Diane Samuels

First produced by the Soho Theatre Company at the Cockpit Theatre in 1993, and at the Vaudeville Theatre in 1996. Between 1938 and 1939 nearly ten thousand children, mostly Jewish, were sent from Germany to Britain. One of these children, EVA Schlesinger, arrives in Manchester, expecting her parents to join her later. When her parents fail to escape the holocaust she changes her name to Evelyn and begins the process of becoming an English schoolgirl . . .

In this scene EVA is at the window of a railway carriage surrounded by other refugees, waving goodbye to her mother and father as the train moves out of the station. From then on she passes through the German border and on to Holland. We see her leaning over the rail of the boat bound for England and finally disembarking at Harwich.

Published by Nick Hern Books Ltd, London

EVA

(*On the train bound for England*) Mutti! Vati! Hello! See. I did get into the carriage. I said I would. See, I'm not crying. I said I wouldn't. I can't open the window! It's sealed tight! Why've you taken your gloves off? You're knocking too hard. Your knuckles are going red! What? I can't hear you! (*Train noise*) Louder! Louder! What! I can't hear! I can't . . . See you in England. (*The train starts to move. EVA sits down*) I mustn't stare at that cross-eyed boy. What if he talks to me? (*A young child starts to cry*) You mustn't cry. There's no point. Stop it! . . . We'll all see our muttis and vatis soon enough . . . And don't look at that cross-eyed boy. (*The crying continues. EVA starts to sing*)

> Hoppe, hoppe Reiter/Wenn er fällt dann schreit er/
> Fällt er in den Graben/Fressen ihn die Raben
> (*Hop hop hop hop Rider/Do not fall beside her/
> If into the ditch you fall/The Ratman gets you all*)

(*Announcing to everyone in the train*) Did any of you know? In England all the men have pipes and look like Sherlock Holmes and everyone has a dog. It's the border! The border! Can't get us now! We're out! Out! Stuff your stupid Hitler!

(*Sounds of train stopping. EVA is eating greedily*) You know what? That dutch lady said we can have as many cakes as we want. And sweets. And lemonade. I'm going to stuff my pockets for later. Who says it's naughty? They all want us to be happy, don't they? Well, that's what I'm doing. Making myself happy.

(*Sound of ship's horn*) You know what? If you lick your lips you'll taste the salt. Sea salt. What d'you mean, Hook of Holland? It can't be. It's nothing like one. It isn't. Look at it. How's that a hook? (*Coughing*) Excuse me . . . (*About to be sick*) . . . it won't come . . . No, I'm fine . . . Really . . . It's just nothing . . . Nothing will come out of me.

(*Ship's horn*) This is Harwich, you know. It really is England . . . (*Sounds of disembarkation*) Can you go through just like that? Don't they search you? (*She picks up a penny*) A penny. They have big money here. It must be a sign of good luck.

Princess Irene
(Young)

The Princess and the Goblin

A Children's Play by Stuart Paterson
From the book by George MacDonald

First performed by the Dundee Repertory Company in 1993. This is
the story of a kind but wayward princess, who having run away
from her strict nurse is captured by Crown Prince Krankl, heir to
the Goblin Kingdom.

This scene takes place in the goblin palace, deep under the
mountain. IRENE thinks she has escaped from Krankl, but he
suddenly appears, accompanied by Fannon, a small dragon.
Krankl announces that he intends to marry her and that one day
she will be Queen of the goblins. IRENE recognises Fannon as the
dragon she had once helped when he hurt his wing. She begs
Krankl to take the dragon away, knowing that whatever she asks he
will do exactly the opposite. Left alone she approaches Fannon,
who at first lets out a tremendous roar.

IRENE

(*To Krankle*) Go! Please go . . . but I ask one favour – take that horrible dragon with you! . . . I hate him. He's ugly and fierce and he scares me . . . (*Krankl exits*) I knew if I asked for one thing, he would do the other. All cruel people are the same . . . You're a good dragon, aren't you? (*Fannon roars fiercely*) Don't be angry, Fannon . . . (*He roars more loudly, comes towards her menacingly*) Fannon? You do remember me, don't you? (*Fannon charges at her, roaring, flailing his wings*) Fannon! Stop it! Please! (*She covers her eyes in terror, but Fannon rushes past her and flushes out Sly who has been hiding*) The goblin spy! (*Fannon chases Sly*) Good boy, Fannon! Chase him! Bite his legs! Go on! (*She watches as Fannon chases Sly off*) Come back, Fannon! Don't leave me here on my own! Let him go. Please, come back. (*Enter Fannon*) Good dragon. I thought you had forgotten me . . . We are friends, aren't we? (*Fannon gives a gentle roar*) Come over here, then. Come on. (*He goes to her and she strokes and pats him*) Let me see your wing. (*She examines his wing*) It's nearly all better now. Soon you'll be able to fly. You really are the best dragon in the whole world . . . And your wings are so beautiful. Perhaps one day you will let me sit on your back and we'll fly over oceans, forests and mountains . . . But remember and pretend to be fierce! (*She roars*) (*Fannon licks her*) Stop licking! I'm glad I've found a friend. It's like I've been swallowed down into the belly of some huge monster . . . But you! You've been a prisoner in the dark for six years. Do you ever dream of the sun? Do you dream of a ball of fire hanging in the sky like a giant lamp? You keep dreaming, Fannon, and I'll take you out of here. I'll find a way, I promise! (*Looks off*) He's coming back! Quickly, pretend to be fierce! As fierce as you can!

Mr Fox

Fantastic Mr Fox

Roald Dahl

Adapted by Sally Reid

First presented in Easter Term 1987 by children and staff of St. Andrew's Primary School, Buckland, Monachorum, Devon.

Three farmers, Bean, Boggis and Bunce are determined to get rid of MR FOX and his young family. They have already shot off MR FOX's beautiful tail and now they have brought in tractors and mechanical shovels to dig them out.

In this scene, set in a tunnel made by the foxes, Mr Badger and his young son have come to complain on behalf of all the other animals living underground, that they are unable to get out of their homes to look for food. They are blaming the foxes for their plight. But the fantastic MR FOX tells them he has devised a cunning plan.

Published by Puffin Books, London

MR FOX

(*Conspiratorially to Mr Badger*) Do you know where we've just been?
. . . Right inside Boggis's Chicken House Number One! . . . Yes! But
that is nothing to where we are going now . . . This way, Badger, old
chap. (*Turns and points to stage right with back to Badger*) . . . Don't
talk about my tail, *please*. It's a painful subject. Nose down, and
DIG. (*They dig along stage towards stage right – feel imaginary floor-
boards above head*) If I am not mistaken, my dear Badger (*whispering*),
we are now underneath the farm which belongs to that nasty little
pot-bellied dwarf, Bunce. We are, in fact, directly underneath the
most INTERESTING part of that farm. (*Puts his head through
imaginary floorboard*) Yes, I've done it again! I've hit it smack on the
nose. Right in the bull's-eye. Come and look! (*They scramble out*)
This, my dear old Badger, is Bunce's Mighty Storehouse! All his
finest stuff is stored here before he sends it off to market. Just feast
your eyes on *that*. What do you think of it, eh? Pretty good grub.
(*Badger and three young foxes run to grab at food*) Stop! This is *my*
party, so *I* shall do the choosing. We mustn't overdo it. Mustn't give
the game away! Mustn't let them know what we've been up to. We
must be neat and tidy and just take a few of the choicest morsels.
So, to start with we shall have four plump young ducks! (*Reaches up
for four from the shelf*) Oh, how lovely and fat they are. No wonder
Bunce gets a special price for them in the market. All right, Badger,
lend me a hand to get them down. You children can help as well . . .
There we go . . . Goodness me, look how your mouths are watering
. . . Gently does it . . . that's the way . . . And what about a couple
of nice smoked hams . . . I adore smoked ham, don't you, Badger?
. . . Worry me? What? . . . All this stealing? . . . (*Arm around Mr
Badger*) My dear old furry frump, do you know anyone in the *whole
world* who wouldn't swipe a few chickens if his children were
starving to death? (*Pause as Mr Badger thinks*) You are far too
respectable.

Flibberty
(A goblin)

Flibberty and the Penguin

David Wood

First presented at The Swan Theatre, Worcester by the Worcester Repertory Company in 1971.

A young penguin has come from Iceland to find his mother and father and meets up with FLIBBERTY, a friendly goblin who helps him in his search.

At the opening of the play, set in a clearing in the Forest, the penguin comes in carrying a small suitcase. He sits down underneath a tree and falls asleep. As he dozes, an acorn drops down on his head and wakes him up. Then another and another. He looks up to see FLIBBERTY sitting up in the branches laughing down at him. FLIBBERTY talks to the penguin who is unable to answer, but tries to make him understand, and invites the audience to help him.

Published by Samuel French, London

FLIBBERTY

Hallo!
The Penguin does not answer, but sadly rubs the top of his head
I didn't hurt you, did I? They're only acorns.
The Penguin nods as FLIBBERTY *jumps down from the tree and comes up to him*
I'm sorry. Look, I'm Flibberty.
The Penguin puts his head on one side enquiringly
Flibberty. Well, Flibberty Gibbet, really, but that's too long for anyone to remember, so everyone calls me Flibberty. I'm a goblin. What are you?
The Penguin points to himself, but makes no reply
Yes, but what *are* you?
The Penguin shrugs his shoulders, points to his beak, and shakes his head
What's the matter? Can't you speak?

The Penguin shakes his head
Oh dear! You poor thing. That must make life very difficult for you.
I mean, I don't even know what you are. I've never seen anything
like . . . (*Noticing the audience, he speaks to them*) You don't know what
he is, do you?
Audience participation
A what? A Penguin? (*To the Penguin*) Is that right?
The Penguin nods
Where have you come from?
The Penguin mimes being very cold, slapping himself to keep warm
(*To the audience*) What's he saying? He looks cold, doesn't he?
Where? Iceland? (*To the Penguin*) Is that right?
The Penguin nods
(*To the audience*) Oh, well done! (*To the Penguin*) How did you get
from Iceland all the way here?
The Penguin mimes 'walking'. The audience shout this out
You walked?
The Penguin nods, then mimes 'swimming'
And swam across the sea?
The Penguin nods, then mimes 'climbing mountains'
And climbed mountains? My, no wonder you look tired. But why
have you come here, to this forest?
The Penguin mimes 'searching for someone'
Looking for someone?
The Penguin mimes 'not one person, two people'
Two people. (*To the audience*) Who could they be?
The Penguin opens his case and takes out a photo of his father and mother
Who are they? (*Helped by the audience*) Your mother and father?
The Penguin nods
Well, where are they?
The Penguin shrugs his shoulders
Where? Oh, you don't know. Of course, that's why you're looking
for them. What happened to them?
The Penguin mimes 'I don't know, they just disappeared'
What? They disappeared?
The Penguin nods and begins to sob
And you've come all this way to find them?
The Penguin nods, sobbing
Oh! (*To the audience*) Well, I think we ought to help him, don't you?
(*To Penguin*) Come on, let's start looking for your father and mother.

James

James and the Giant Peach
Roald Dahl
Adapted by Richard R. George

Written in 1961 and adapted as a play in 1982 by American school teacher, Richard George.

JAMES has escaped from his dreadful guardians, Aunt Spiker and Aunt Sponge and sets off inside the Giant Peach on his amazing adventures. He is accompanied by his friends, Earthworm, Centipede, Old-Green-Grasshopper, Spider, Ladybird and Glow-Worm.

In this scene, the Peach has broken through the garden fence, rolled down the hill and on and on towards Dover, where it hurtles over the white cliffs and into the sea. Now it is floating further and further out, bobbing along on the waves. JAMES and his friends have climbed out and are sitting on top of it, when the Centipede looks towards the horizon and sees a thin black thing moving towards them. It is a shark. Soon there are more sharks and they begin to attack the Peach. Ladybird appeals to JAMES. Surely he can think of something before they are all eaten alive.

Published by Puffin Books, London

JAMES

There *is* something that I believe we might try. I'm not saying it'll work . . . I . . . I . . . I'm afraid it's no good . . . after all . . . (*Shaking his head*) I'm terribly sorry. I forgot. We don't have any string. We'd need hundreds of yards of string to make this work . . . The Silkworm? You can wake him up and make him spin? And you, Spider, can spin just as well as any Silkworm! Can you make enough between you? And would it be strong? . . . I'm going to lift this Peach clear out of the water! With seagulls! the place is full of them. Look up there! (*Pointing towards the sky*) I'm going to take a long silk string and I'm going to loop one end of it around a seagull's neck. And then I'm going to tie the other end to the stem of the Peach. (*JAMES points to the Peach stem, which is standing up like a mast in the middle of the stage*) Then I'm going to get another seagull and do the same thing again, and then another and another . . . there's no shortage of seagulls. Look for yourself. We'll probably need four hundred, five hundred . . . maybe even a thousand . . . I don't know . . . I shall simply go on hooking them up to the stem until we have enough to lift us. It's like balloons. You give someone enough balloons to hold, I mean *really* enough, then up he goes. And a seagull has far more lifting power than a balloon. If only we have *time* to do it . . . We'll do it with bait. With a worm, of course. Seagulls love worms, didn't you know that? And luckily for us, we have here the biggest, fattest, juiest Earthworm . . . The seagulls have already spotted him. That's why there are so many of them circling around. But they daren't come down and get him while all the rest of us are standing here. So this is what we'll do . . . (*He puts his arm around Earthworm*) I won't let them *touch* you. I promise I won't! But we've got to hurry! Look down there! Action stations! There's not a moment to lose! All hands below deck except Earthworm!

Edmund

The Lion, the Witch and the Wardrobe

C.S. Lewis

Dramatised by Adrian Mitchell

First performed in 1998 at the Royal Shakespeare Theatre, Stratford-upon-Avon and transferred to the Barbican Theatre, London in 1999.

This is the story of four children, Lucy, Susan, Peter and EDMUND, who are evacuated to the country during the London Blitz. Exploring the attic in their new home they discover an old wardrobe – the gateway opening out into the Land of Narnia. Narnia is under a spell, and the four children soon find themselves caught up in an adventure that leads to a final struggle between the powers of good and evil – the Lion, Aslan and the wicked White Witch. EDMUND is the first to meet the White Witch, She wraps him in her fur mantle, feeds him Turkish Delight and makes him promise to bring the other children to see her.

This scene is set in the courtyard of the Witch's house at night. EDMUND enters cautiously. There are shadowy figures of people and animals all around him – standing very still. He cowers away from an enormous lion, crouched and ready to spring, then realises it is only a statue – the statue of the great Aslan.

Published by Oberon Books, London

EDMUND

A lion! (*EDMUND cowers away from an enormous lion crouched as if it is ready to spring*) Why's it standing so still? (*He ventures a little nearer*) Hey, its head's all covered in snow. Only a statue. (*He walks forward and touches the lion's head, very quickly*) Cold stone! So this is the great Lion Aslan! The Queen's turned him into stone. So *that's* the end of all their fine ideas! (*He takes a stub of pencil out of his pocket and scribbles a moustache and spectacles on the lion's head*) Who's afraid of Aslan? Yah! Stupid old Aslan! How do you like being a statue? (*EDMUND moves on across the courtyard among stone statues of satyrs, wolves, bears, foxes and cat-a-mountains and dryads and a centaur and a winged horse and a dragon. Right in the middle stands a stone giant. EDMUND moves past the giant gingerly towards stone steps leading to a doorway from which a pale light shines. Across the threshold lies a great wolf*) It's all right – only a stone wolf. It couldn't hurt a flea.

But as EDMUND raises his leg to step over the wolf, the huge creature rises and opens its mouth and speaks in a growling voice. It is Maugrim the wolf, head of the Witch's Secret Police.

(*Trembling*) If you please, sir. My name is Edmund, and I'm the Son of Adam Her Majesty met in the wood the other day and I've come to bring her the news that my brother and sisters are now in Narnia – quite close, at the Beavers' house. She – she wanted to see them. Who are you, sir? . . . [*Maugrim: I am Maugrim, the Chief of the Queen's Secret Police*] . . . Will you tell Her Majesty I am here? . . . (*Maugrim vanishes into the house. EDMUND stands very still*) It's hard to stand still when you're trembling. I mustn't be afraid. Try to think about something nice . . . ah, yes . . . Turkish Delight . . . Turkish Delight . . . (*Maugrim comes bounding out of the house and escorts EDMUND in through the stone doorway. On the throne, lit by a single lamp, sits the Witch. Maugrim escorts EDMUND towards her. EDMUND bows to the Witch*) (*Eagerly*) I've come, your Majesty . . . Please, your Majesty, I've done the best I can. They're in Mr and Mrs Beaver's house . . . The Beaver says – Aslan is on the move . . . They're going to meet him at the Stone Table . . . that's what the Beaver said . . . Please, your Majesty, I didn't have much lunch. Could I have some Turkish Delight?

The Pied Piper

The Pied Piper
Adrian Mitchell

First performed at the National Theatre in 1986 and set in the Market Place in Hamelin Town.

In this scene, the stage darkens and we hear squeakings and shufflings. Red eyes are glowing in the dark. The town band enters with a small boy limping behind the procession. Then the PIED PIPER appears, dressed as a Mystery Tramp. He plays a spectacular solo on his pipe (if possible) and eventually, after an acrobatic solo, sits exhausted, then notices the audience.

Published by Samuel French, London

PIPER

Good morning! Good grief! We haven't met, have we! Some folk call me – The Mystery Tramp. But they're wrong. This is just my Mystery Tramp disguise. As Mr Robert Browning says in his famous poem:

> I chiefly use my piping charm
> On creatures that do people harm,
> The mole and toad and newt and viper;
> And people call me – (*pauses to think*)

(*Audience: The Pied Piper!*)

Shh! Yes, the Pied Piper. If people know who I really am they bother me blue. 'Please Mr Piper, please, please, please! There's bugs in our rugs and lice in our rice and fleas all over Auntie Louise!' Thing is, I'm tired to me teeth with pest control! I fancy retiring to a very comfortable mountain round here. Called the Koppelburg . . . (*He addresses the Baron and the Mayoress*) Know anything about rats? I was more or less brought up with them. Kept a dozen pet rats when I was a lad . . . Took 'em to school to keep teacher amused . . . Bite me? Bless me, of course they did. It's in the nature of your rat to bite . . . Some were bad and none of them good. The barn rat's not so grisly, he's a plump little fellow, living off top of the wheat and dairymilk. He gives you a nice clean little nip. But your sewer rat, he's a different kettle of germs, he is. Nastly class of bite, three-cornered bite, bleeds for ever such a long time . . . I've been bitten thousands of times, on account of me being so tasty. You see this thumbnail, bitten right through ten years ago and still got a split in it. That was the worst bite I ever got bit. The pain went shooting all the way up to my ear. Me thumb went black and I was told I ought to have it taken off, but I kept it cos I was fond of it. Had it all me life, you know. (*Sucks thumb*). . . Can I rid Hamelin of rats? . . . Yes – easy as pie . . . You'll have no rats tomorrow . . . Fifty quid cash, is that fair? . . . One thousand golden pounds – . . . In a silken purse? Right, if that's the going rate I won't say no, on account of me being poor . . . It's a deal.

Peter
(Aged 10)

The Railway Children
E. Nesbit

First published in 1906 and more than fifty years later made into a BBC Children's Television series – and finally a feature film.

Three children, Bobbie, PETER and Phyllis, lived happily in their comfortable London house, until one day some men came and took away their father. Their Mother was left with very little money and they were forced to go and live in a not very nice house in the country. A railway line ran nearby, and in those days there were lots of things to do beside a railway. All sorts of people travelled by train – and 'the Railway Children' made friends with some of them.

They find a young boy lying in the tunnel with a broken leg and run for help. They bring him home and their mother puts him to bed and calls the doctor. In this scene they are waiting downstairs in the parlour, listening to the sounds of the doctor overhead and the groans of his patient. The girls are very distressed, but PETER finds it all very exciting. He teases the girls, and despite their protests suggests a game of bone-setting. This gives Bobbie and Phyllis their opportunity for revenge.

Published by Penguin Books, London

PETER

It *is* horrible, but it's very exciting. I wish doctors weren't so stuck up about who'll they'll have in the room when they're doing things. I should most awfully like to see a leg set. I believe the bones crunch like anything . . . How are you going to be Red Cross Nurses, like you were talking of coming home, if you can't even stand hearing me say about bones crunching? You'd have to *hear* them crunch on the field of battle – and be steeped in gore up to the elbows . . . It would be a jolly good thing for you if I were to talk to you every day for half an hour about broken bones and people's insides, so as to get you used to it . . . I'll tell you what they do, they strap the broken man down so that he can't resist or interfere with their doctorish designs, and then someone holds his head, and someone holds his leg – the broken one, and pulls it till the bones fit in – with a crunch, mind you! Then they strap it up and – let's play at bone-setting! . . . I'll get the splints and bandages, you get the couch of suffering ready. (*He fetches ropes and two boards for splints*) Now, then. (*He lies down on the settle, groaning most grievously*) Not so tight. You'll break my other leg . . . That's enough, I can't move at all. Oh my poor leg! . . . Shall we play it's bleeding freely . . . (*The girls move away leaving* PETER *tied up*) . . . You beasts! (*He tries to free himself*) I'll yell, and Mother will come!

Charlotte
(A spider)

Charlotte's Web

E.B. White
Adapted by Joseph Robinette

This play tells the story of a little girl called Fern, who with the help of CHARLOTTE, an extraordinary spider, saves her pet pig Wilbur form the usual fate of nice fat little pigs.

Wilbur, who is by now five weeks old, has been sent to live with Fern's Uncle, Homer Zuckerman. He is being fed lots of lovely 'slops' and Fern is allowed to visit him whenever she wants. The farm animals come to visit him too, including an old Sheep and her Lamb, a rat named Templeton and CHARLOTTE, who lives in her web in the corner of the barn. Wilbur is very happy until one day the old Sheep tells him that Zuckerman is fattening him up so that he can kill him and turn him into bacon.

In this scene CHARLOTTE promises to save Wilbur.

Published by The Dramatic Publishing Company, Ilinois

CHARLOTTE

[*WILBUR: Were you serious when you promised you would keep them from killing me?*] . . . (*CHARLOTTE*) I've never been more serious in my life . . . But I want you to get plenty of sleep and stop worrying. (*Wilbur stretches out on the straw as the lights begin to dim*) Good night, Wilbur (*A pause*) . . . Good night. (*The barn is now in shadows. Wilbur falls asleep*) What to do. What to do. I promised to save his life, and I am determined to keep that promise. But how? (*A pause*) Wait a minute. The way to save Wilbur is to play a trick on Zuckerman. If I can fool a bug, I can surely fool a man. People are not as smart as bugs. (*A beat*) Of course. That's it. This will not be easy, but it must be done. First, I tear a section out of the web and leave an open space in the middle. Now, I shall weave new threads to take the place of the ones I removed. (*She chants slightly*) Swing spinnerets. Let out the thread. The longer it gets, the better it's read. (*She begins to 'write' with elaborate movements*) Atta girl. Attach. Pay out line. Descend. Complete the curve. Easy now. That's it. Back up. Take your time. Now tie it off. Good. (*She chants*) The message is spun. I've come to the end. The job that I've done is all for my friend. (*She steps aside as a special light reveals the words 'Some Pig' written in the web*) (*She reads aloud*) Some pig. (*She smiles*) Not bad, old girl, for the first time around. But it *was* quite exhausting. I'd better catch a little nap before daybreak. (*She exits behind the web*)

Lucy

Invisible Friends

Alan Ayckbourn

First performed in 1989 at the Stephen Joseph Theatre, Scarborough, the play is about a very ordinary girl called LUCY. With her father glued to the telly, her mother preoccupied with local gossip and her brother, known as 'Grisly Gary' shut up in his room listening to heavy metal music, no one wants to know about her place in the school swimming team. So LUCY revives her child-hood fantasy friend, Zara. Only this time, Zara materialises, bringing with her an idealised father and brother, and showing her how to make her real family vanish.

In this scene, LUCY has just come out of Gary's bedroom having failed to make him listen to her, as she tries to tell him her good news above the sound of the stereo. She enters her own room and introduces the audience to her invisible friend, Zara.

Published by Faber & Faber, London

ZARA

You may have heard my mum talking about my invisible friend. Do you remember? Well, that's my invisible friend, Zara. (*Introducing her*) This is Zara. I want you to meet Zara. Zara, say hallo. That's it. Will you say hallo to Zara, my invisible friend? I invented Zara – oh, years ago – when I was seven or eight. Just for fun. I think I was ill at that time and wasn't allowed to play with any of my real friends, so I made up Zara. She's my special friend that no one can see except me. Of course, I can't really see her either. Not really. Although sometimes I . . . It's almost as if I could see her, sometimes. If I concentrate very hard it's like I can just glimpse her out of the corner of my eye. (*She is thoughtful for a second*) Still. Anyway. I've kept Zara for years and years. Until they all started saying I was much too old for that sort of thing and got worried and started talking about sending for a doctor. So then I didn't take her round with me quite so much after that. But she's still here. And when I feel really sad and depressed like I do today, then I sit and talk to Zara. Zara always understands. Zara always listens. She's special. Aren't you, Zara? (*She listens to Zara*) What's that? Yes, I wish he'd turn his music down, too. I've asked him, haven't I? (*Mimicking Gary*) 'How can I hear it if I turn it down, I can't hear the bass then, can I?' I used to have pictures in here but every time he put a disc on they fell off the walls. (*Pause. The music continues*) I mean, don't get me wrong. We like loud music, don't we, Zara? We love loud music. Sometimes. (*Yelling*) BUT NOT ALL THE TIME.

(*Pause*)

Why doesn't he ever listen to quiet music? Just once. Wouldn't that be nice? . . . But if he did that, he wouldn't be Grisly Gary then, would he?

(*Pause*)

Oh, Zara, did I tell you I've been picked for the school swimming team? Isn't that exciting? Yes. Thank you. I'm glad you're excited, too. Good.

(*Pause*)

(*Shouting*) IF ANYONE IS INTERESTED AT ALL, I WAS PICKED FOR THE SCHOOL SWIMMING TEAM TODAY. WHAT ABOUT THAT, FOLKS?

(*She listens. No reply*)

Great. Thanks for your support, everyone. (*Tearful*) They might at least . . . They could have at least . . . Oh, Zara . . . I know you're always here, but sometimes I get so . . . lonely . . .

(*She sits on her bed, sad, angry and frustrated*)

Suzy

Mr A's Amazing Maze Plays

Alan Ayckbourn

First performed at the Stephen Joseph Theatre in the Round, Scarborough in 1988.

SUZY lives in a small cottage with her mother and her dog, Neville – her father went up in a hot air balloon one day and never came back down. Except for missing SUZY's father they are all quite happy, until the suave Mr Accousticus moves into the mysterious old house across from their cottage and sweeps Mother off her feet.

Mr Accousticus hates noise, and since his arrival, Neville has lost his bark and their friend and neighbour, Mr Passerby, has lost his operatic voice.

While Mr Accousticus is having supper with Mother, SUZY and Neville plan to get into his house and search for Neville's bark and Mr Passerby's operatic voice. They creep through the garden and along the path till they reach the big front door. Neville pushes it open and they find themselves in a dark hallway. At this point in the play it is up to the audience to choose which course SUZY and Neville should take, and the search sequence begins.

In this scene SUZY and Neville have found their way into Mr Accousticus's Music Room. From there they progress to the Dining Room and then on into the Conservatory.

Published by Samuel French, London

SUZY

(SUZY and Neville enter the Music Room) This must be the music room. Look, a piano. (She tries a few notes) Well, I think it's a piano. Here's a harp. (She tries a few notes – Neville finds a tin whistle) What have you got there? A whistle? (Neville tries to blow it) Sshh! Let's try that door. It's the only way out of here. (She tries it, but it is locked) What's this say? (She reads something on the door) 'I won't let you in to dine. Eat my food or drink my wine/Taste my breakfast, sip my tea/'Til you've sung a song for me.' Oh, terrific! Does that mean we have to sing to open the door? I suppose it does. You can't sing, can you, Neville, poor old thing. Wait a minute. I can't think of any songs. I know – what about the one that Mr Passerby always used to sing . . . ?

> (*She sings*) Early one morning . . .
> Just as the sun was rising . . . that's it . . .

(SUZY *has difficulty in remembering the words*)

> I heard a maiden singing in the valley below.
> Oh, don't deceive me,
> Oh, never leave me,
> How could you treat a poor maiden so?

(*At the end of all this the door opens*) Look, Neville, it worked! Come on, then. Dinner is served. (SUZY *and Neville enter the Dining Room*) I wouldn't like to eat in here very much. Not on my own. And it's so dusty. You'd get mouthfuls of fluff. (*They examine things on the table*) Ugggh! Well, it doesn't look as if anyone's even been in here for years, let alone eaten in here. On we go then. We could try those windows. They seem to open and lead to somewhere. Yes, it's full of huge plants out there. It's like a jungle. I think it's what they call a conservatory. Shall we go out there, Neville? It looks rather dangerous . . . What have you found, then? Oh, yes. It's a little concealed door. It's painted like the wall so you hardly notice it. Oh dear. Another choice. Which way shall we go then? Through this door? . . . Or through the French windows and into the jungle? . . . (SUZY *and Neville step out through the windows and into the conservatory*) I hope there aren't any wild animals in here . . . Like tigers. Or snakes. I don't like snakes at all. It is very thick, the undergrowth, though. You can hardly see where you're going. Neville? . . . (*Neville has somehow lost sight of* SUZY. *And now* SUZY *has lost Neville*) Neville? Don't be silly, Neville. Don't play games. We haven't got time for that. If Mr Accousticus comes back while we're here, we're in real trouble. Neville . . . Neville? (*They prowl about for a bit. Then Neville leaps out at* SUZY, *mistaking her for someone else. They roll about*) Neville, stop it! It's me! It's me! Neville! (*Neville stops attacking her*) Don't ever do that again. I thought you were a tiger . . . Now, how do we get out of here? If we ever do get out. What's that in the corner over there? It looks like a door . . . (*She moves over to it*) Yes, look, Neville. It's the door to a lift. Come on, let's try the lift . . .

Gaby

The Siege

Adrian Mitchell

First published in 1996, this play was commissioned by the National Playwright Commissioning Group especially for performance in schools.

The Swados family – Eduardo, an office clerk married to Sally, a hospital nurse; and their children, Mike, twins Arlo and Betsy, Lucy, Karl and Elli – live in the peaceful town of Arden, a town much like any town in England. War breaks out and they are under siege by the forces of the province of Dower. The government is toppling and is taken over by a plausible racist gangster called Doctor Jameson.

In this scene the people of the town have been queuing up for bread. A young friend of Betsy's – GABY – steps forward and talks directly to the audience, describing what life is like living in an air raid shelter.

Published by Oberon Books, London

GABY

I dunno if you've ever been in an air raid. Just in case you get caught in one, I'll tell you what to do. First, stick yourself down a shelter. Best thing is to be in a cellar near home with friends and some family. Winter you go for months on end without ever taking off all your clothes. You never see your own body. You know it's turning into something skinny and horrible. You want to forget about it. But it itches and it aches, just to remind you it's there. And of course, it smells. But you get used to your own smell and the smell of your friends and family. Smell a stranger a mile off. (*Sniffs, laughs*) There's a lot of boredom in air raids. You read a book, if you can get near enough the lamp. Maybe you play cards for a tin of sardines. And there's always somebody saying the same old stupid things . . . (*All Clear sounds*) Then the All Clear sounds. And there's always the same old argument: Do you pack up the blankets and the kids and go upstairs? Or stop in the cellar and wait for the next raid? Look, sometimes it's real fun down the shelter. Yeah. And we all sing old Beatles songs and stuff. Right? But sometimes there's a kid missing and there's screaming outside and it feels like you're stuck down in hell and you know that hell is a cold dark place where little children die. (*Turns and walks away*)

Angela
(Manchester – aged 11-12)

Six Primroses Each

Ellen Dryden

Presented by the Chiswick Youth Theatre in workshop and performance between 1985 and 1991, and set in a Church Hall in the country during World War II (1940).

In this opening scene a group of children are waiting around in the Church Hall. They have been evacuated from the East End of London because of the bombing and are about to be allocated to various homes near by. They are homesick and apprehensive, but are trying to make the best of things. ANGELA, a bouncy north country girl, comes in with her side-kick, Janet. She is not an evacuee like the others, and is staying with her Auntie in the country until the air raids are over in Manchester. She is most unwelcoming.

From: *Six Primroses Each and Other Plays for Young Actors*
Published by First Writes Publications, London

ANGELA

Oh, hello! I didn't know there was anybody in here! (*Of course she did. That's why she's come in*) They must have forgotten about you . . . (*She looks them up and down*) I don't think you ought to sit on the chairs. Not till you've been disinfected! . . . No! I'm not an *evacuee*! I'm here with my Auntie Joan to pick out a couple of you. She's in there talking to Miss Deacon. They probably put you in here 'cos they think you've got nits. Or fleas. (*Janet giggles*) Or ringworm or something like that! . . . It's something dirty people get. Your hair all comes out in little round patches. A lot of the scruffy lot from London get it. They paint your head purple . . . I expect they're saving you for Mrs Fitz-Hughes at the Manor. She always takes a load of scruffy ones. They never stay long though! She's got a row of little camp beds in the stables and she makes the evacuees do all the work. Scrub the floors, clean out the pigsties, muck out the hens and black-lead all the grates. And if she has Catholics she makes them eat meat on Fridays, and she made David Goldberg eat a pig's brains – and he was sick all over and she sent him back. And she gives you bread and milk all the time. With stale bread, and she waters the milk. And no sugar. And the Major – that's her husband – he's too old to be a proper soldier – he lets us go on nature walks on his land. And he said we could pick primroses. '*The children can pick six each with one leaf, and the Teachers can pick twelve with two leaves.*' And it's freezing . . . And you have to go to church on Sunday. Or Chapel . . . It's dead funny in Chapel. My Auntie Joan goes. And the man next door hates the Chapel, and he killed his pig on a Sunday morning! We were just singing the first hymn when it started squealing its head off 'cos it knew what he was going to do, and he chased it all round the garden and it squealed and squealed and then it was quiet – and everybody looked at each other 'cos they knew he'd cut its throat and it was bleeding to death . . . (*A voice is heard from outside*) Oh that's my Auntie Joan! Come on Janet. Well I shouldn't think I'll see you lot again. (*With pride*) And it just so happens that Manchester is a very important industrial city, – with Docks and the Ship Canal. It's just as important as rotten old London!

Mildred Hubble
(Aged 11)

The Worst Witch

Adapted by Paul Todd from Jill Murphy's books

The Worst Witch series of books, the first of which was published in 1975, toured nationally as a musical with book, music and lyrics by Paul Todd with Jill Murphy in 1991/2, and has recently been made into a children's series for Carlton TV.

MILDRED HUBBLE is 'The Worst Witch' at Miss Cackle's Academy for Witches – she always gets things wrong. But she manages to get by until Ethel, the teacher's pet, becomes her deadly enemy. In this scene MILDRED has been summoned to Miss Cackle's office to explain a recent incident. She is very nervous and hoping desperately that she won't be expelled.

Published by Puffin Books, London

MILDRED

Mildred Headle, Hubmistress. I mean Hubble, Headmistress. Mildred Hubble . . . Like 'trouble', Miss, yes. Unfortunately . . . Except there's no 'o' in it . . . But there are two 'b's . . And an 'h' instead of 't', 'r'. Obviously. (*Pause*) You can borrow my pen, Miss, if yours has run out . . . Why am I here? Now, that's a very good question. I've not done anything wrong . . . much. At all, really. It's a lot of fuss about nothing, if you ask me . . . Didn't you? Oh, I'm sorry. (*She giggles nervously*) I am taking it seriously, Miss Cackle. Very, very seriously (*she giggles again*). Sorry. It was Miss Hardbroom. And a Spelling mistake, that's all. A silly, little Spelling mistake in Miss Hardbroom's class . . . I turned Ethel into a pig. That was the mistake. It was meant to be a frog. I've got to have extra lessons. They're really, really complicated, all the animal spells, aren't they? . . . Right. Well, it all started when I was given a tabby instead of a black cat – I mean, everyone else got a black cat and H.B. – I mean, Miss Hardbroom – probably did it on purpose, but Tabby's lovely and really intelligent and things, but Ethel made fun of him and I didn't like it 'cos he can't answer back, and Ethel said that we were both as bad as each other (but she didn't say what at!) so I said: 'You'd better be quiet' and she said 'Won't!' and I said 'If you don't, I'll –' and she said 'What?' and I said I'd turn her into a frog and she said I couldn't 'cos I didn't know the spell. So I did. Well, I didn't. I nearly did. But I've changed her back. She's a bit disgruntled but she's alright. Apart from the occasional oink . . . Witches' Code, Rule Number Seven Paragraph Two . . .? (*Pause*) No, I'm afraid that escapes me at present . . . 'It is not customary . . . '? Oh, yes! 'It is not customary to practise tricks on your fellows' . . . No, Miss, I won't forget in future . . . Can I? Really? I can go? I thought I was going to be – (*Pause*) You're right. The extra lessons with H.B. – Hardbroom'll be punishment enough. Thank you, Miss Cackle. (*She starts to exit, then turns*) When you were little? Extra Chanting lessons? Really? (*Pause*) For two whole terms? (*Pause*) I won't tell a soul. Honestly. Not a word. Goodbye, Miss Cackle. And thank you. I'll see you soon. (*Re-considering*) I didn't mean that. At least I hope I didn't. (*Moving off, to herself*) Well, well, well . . . who would've thought Miss Cackle was ever a little girl . . .?

Marcus
(Aged 12-13)

The Children's Ward

Ellen Dryden

Presented by the Chiswick Youth Theatre in workshop and performance between 1985 and 1991, this award-winning short play is set in the children's ward of a large modern hospital.

MARCUS is a lively, energetic long-stay patient. His mother and little brother have come to visit him in the Playroom, but he has retreated back into the ward to get away from them. He sits on his bed talking to two other patients: Chris, who is building a model village which MARCUS's brother has been 'mucking about with', and Patrick, who has just been admitted with suspected appendicitis.

From: *Six Primroses Each and Other Plays for Young Actors*
Published by First Writes Publications, London

MARCUS

'Lo Chris . . . (*He goes and sits on his bed which is immediately opposite Patrick's*) My little brother's here. He's in the Playroom. That's why I came in here. He's screaming the place down. He wants the little house, he says. My Mum keeps shovelling him into the Wendy House and he keeps kicking the other kids. I wish she wouldn't keep bringing him . . . She spoils him rotten. I tell her not to bring him but she thinks he might get what I've got so she wants him to get used to Hospital . . . There's some horrible kids in this place but he's worse than any of them. My Mum doesn't believe in violence so she never hits him – she goes berserk when I do. And she sits up all night with my Dad discussing my aggressive tendencies and where she's gone wrong. (*He chuckles delightedly*) She goes to consciousness raising groups . . . She's going veggie as well. She cooks these great big panfuls of beans and stuff. Looks like puke. She reckons it's diet why I'm in here. My Dad stops off at Macdonalds on the way home from work and says he's not too hungry when he gets in. So she saves up all the bean stuff and puts some lentils in it and gives it him the next day. Do you know, she won't let me and my brother have any aggressive toys or anything . . . She's trying to find a Save the Whale game for my computer. I can't have nasty War games 'cos she's trying to breed a better sort of boy . . . My brother's the most violent little devil ever. I hate him. He got chucked out of his playgroup last week . . . He set fire to the Wendy House.

Ernie

Ernie's Incredible Illucinations
Alan Ayckbourn

First published in 1969 and set in a Doctor's Surgery and wherever ERNIE's imagination takes him.

ERNIE's Mum and Dad are worried about what they call his 'illucinations' – so worried that they take him to the Doctor. They explain that not only are they concerned for ERNIE, but also for themselves, as he seems to be drawing *them* into his imaginings as well. The Doctor refuses to take this seriously until he too is forced to take part in one of ERNIE's incredible 'illucinations'.

In this scene, ERNIE explains to the Doctor how he managed to involve his Mum and his Auntie May in his 'illucinations', acting out scenes where his home is invaded by soldiers and his Auntie takes part in the world heavyweight boxing contest against 'The Kid'.

Published by Samuel French, London

ERNIE

It started with these daydreams. You know, the sort everybody gets. Where you suddenly score a hat trick in the first five minutes of the Cup Final, or you bowl out the West Indies for ten runs – or saving your granny from a blazing helicopter, all that sort of rubbish. It was one wet Saturday afternoon and me and my mum and dad were all sitting about in the happy home having one of those exciting afternoon rave-ups we usually have in our house. (*ERNIE sits in the Doctor's chair and starts to read a book*) Meanwhile – I was reading a book about the French wartime resistance workers and of the dangers they faced – often arrested in their homes. I started wondering what would happen if a squad of soldiers turned up at our front door, having been tipped off about the secret radio transmitter hidden in our cistern – when suddenly . . . I shouldn't go out there, Mum . . . I said don't go out there . . . It's not the milkman. It's a squad of enemy soldiers . . . They've come for me . . .They've found out about the radio transmitter . . . (*The soldiers charge the door. A loud crash*) Don't go out, Mum . . . Don't go! . . . Mum . . . (*ERNIE stepping forward*) Well, Mum and Dad decided that the best thing to do was to pretend it hadn't happened. That was usually the way they coped with all emergencies . . . And then – Auntie May arrived to stay. I liked my Auntie May. (*Auntie May enters*) . . . And Auntie May took me to the fair . . . Oh, come on Auntie. Let's go in and watch the boxing . . . This way, Auntie . . . Auntie, where are you going? . . . Auntie! (*ERNIE stepping forward*) And then suddenly I got this idea. Maybe Auntie May could be the new heavyweight champion of the world . . . (*The bell rings and Auntie May comes bouncing out of her corner – she bombards the Kid with punches. ERNIE, commentator style*) And Auntie May moves in again and catches the Kid with a left and a right to the body and there's a right-cross to the head – and that really hurt him – and it looks from here as if the champ is in real trouble . . . as this amazing sixty-eight-year-old challenger follows up with a series of sharp left-jabs – one, two, three, four jabs . . . (*The Kid is reeling*) And then, bang, a right-hook and he's down . . . ! (*The Kid goes down on his knees. The crowd cheers . . . The Kid gets up again*) And the Kid's on his feet but he's no idea where he is – and there's that tremendous right upper-cut – and he's down again! . . .

George
(Aged 8)

George's Marvellous Medicine

Roald Dahl

Adapted for stage by Stuart Paterson

First performed by the Borderline Theatre Company in 1990. GEORGE lives in a farmhouse with his Mother and Father and Grandma – a horrible old lady who is particularly horrible to GEORGE, especially when he is left on his own with her.

GEORGE's Mother and Father have gone shopping in the village, leaving GEORGE to take care of Grandma and give her her medicine at eleven o'clock. As soon as she wakes up she is demanding a cup of tea – sending GEORGE backwards and forwards to the kitchen for more sugar, a saucer and then a teaspoon. As she stirs her tea she accuses him of growing too fast. 'Boys who grow too fast are stupid and lazy.' She beckons to GEORGE to come closer to her and starts to tell him about magic powers and 'dark places where dark things live and squirm and slither all over each other . . .' In terror GEORGE runs out into the kitchen and slams the door after him. He is now quite sure that Grandma is a witch. Suddenly he remembers her medicine. If only he could invent a medicine so strong and so fierce that it would either cure her or blow the top of her head right off!

In this scene GEORGE has almost completed his marvellous medicine and is stirring the mixture with a long wooden spoon. A rich blue smoke rises from the surface of the liquid. He inhales deeply, coughs and splutters, then inhales again.

GEORGE

Oh I bet nothing's ever smelled like that before in the whole history of the world, except maybe a witch's big black cauldron. Just one whiff sets your brain on fire and sends prickles down the backs of your legs. (*He shivers, and stirs more quickly, dancing from foot to foot*) I can see sparks flashing in the foam. There it is again – like lightning in a storm! This is wonderful! It's the best, the

best, the best, the best, the best thing ever!
(*He has begun to dance around the steaming pot. Lost in mischief's magic spell, he begins to dance around the kitchen, and chant*)

> Fiery broth and witch's brew
> Foamy froth and riches blue
> Fume and spume and spoondrift spray
> Fizzle swizzle shout hooray
> Watch it sloshing, swashing, sploshing
> Hear it hissing, spissing, squishing
> Grandma better start to pray.

(*Clutching his head*) Calm down, George. I've got to stay calm. (*He takes a deep breath*) I mustn't make any mistakes now. Think, George, think! (*He turns off the flame under the pan*) It'll need plenty of time to cool down (*He waves away the steam, stirs away the froth, and peers in at his medicine*) But it's blue, the deepest blue you've ever seen. It needs more brown! It has to be brown or she'll get suspicious.

(*GEORGE dashes out to the shed*) (*From inside the shed*) Brown paint, brown paint – please let there be brown paint!

(*GEORGE emerges from the shed clutching an old, dirty can. He reads its label*) DARK BROWN GLOSS PAINT – ONE QUART. In it goes! (*He prises off the lid and pours the paint into the saucepan. He stirs the paint gently into the mixture with the long wooden spoon*) It's working! It's all turning brown! A lovely thick creamy brown! . . . I'm coming, Grandma . . . I'm not forgetting you, Grandma. I'm thinking about you all the time . . . (*GEORGE snatches the bottle of Grandma's real medicine from the sideboard, takes out the cork and pours it all down the sink*) We won't be needing you any more. We've got something much better than you! Oh boy, haven't we just! (*He pours the mixture into the medicine bottle and replaces the cork*) I've done it, I've done it! (*He touches the bottle, burns himself*) Ouch! It's still boiling hot, and it's nearly eleven o'clock . . . It won't be long now, Grandma (*Quietly, tense with excitement*) Under the tap – that's it! Under the cold tap! (*He runs cold water from the tap over the bottle*) If only the glass doesn't break. Please, please, don't let the glass break . . . It's cooler already. I can put my hand right round it. (*He keeps the bottle under the cold water*) I think we've done it! I think we've really done it. (*GEORGE turns off the tap and dries the bottle with a dishcloth*) Grandma – it's medicine time!

Albert
(Very young)

In Service

Ellen Dryden

Presented by the Chiswick Youth Theatre in workshop and performance between 1985 and 1991, this short play is set in the attic
and kitchen of a large Victorian house and depicts a day in the life
of young people in service in the 1890s.

It is dawn and two of the maids are already at work in the
scullery, when a third maid, Emily, brings in ALBERT – a small,
wiry, impudent-looking boy – barefoot and covered in mud. She
explains that he is a mudlark, found by the Young Lady of the
house, who has 'a lot of silly ideas about looking after the poor'.
Lavinia, a young nursery maid from the country, is handed a
bucket and brush and ordered to clean up ALBERT. As she does so,
he begins to tell her about his life as a mudlark.

From: *Six Primroses Each and Other Plays for Young Actors*
Published by First Writes Publications, London

ALBERT

You go in up to your knees this weather. I bin in up to me waist. I likes to nip in between the barges as well. That's where you get the best stuff. That's where you get the pitch all over you. Off of the barges . . . the pitch . . . off the bottoms. (*He looks interestedly at his arm*) That's horse muck from the stables that is! . . . In the House of Correction they stood you in the yard and hosed you down. Knocked you off your feet that did . . . Been there four times. I prigged some coal from the barges and they got me. I was looking for copper nails. They're the best but there wasn't none. Prison's all right in the winter. They give you shoes and a shirt. It's powerful hard on the feet in the winter. With the ice . . . And the broken glass. That's bad . . . There look. A broken bottle done that. Sliced through them toes. Still. If you ain't got no toes you can't get no chilblains . . . The mud blocked up the ends and I don't miss them toes now . . . I live back of King James Stairs. Down Wapping Wall. My mum sells fish down there. When she can. But she's been in the Fever Hospital a long time now. My Dad fell between the barges. Broke his back. Drunk as usual. So me and our Nellie went mud-larking. (*Proudly*) I get fourpence a day . . . you can on a good day . . . If I could find a hammer or a saw I could get eightpence then we'd be all right. Will she – the Lady – will she, do you reckon, she'll give me some money? . . . I know reading . . . Well. I did once. One night I was down by the steam factory. The warm water runs out there and you can warm your feet up a bit, you see. These big lads was talking about the ragged school in the High Street. They said it was good fun – you had a good laugh, making game of the master, and that, and putting out the gas and chucking the slates about. They said there was a fire there. So I went along to have a warm. They used to give us tea parties and magic lantern shows. I got to like it so I went every night. They was mostly thieves that used to go. Thieving the coal and cutting the ropes off of the ships and selling it at the rag shops. We all used to go thieving after School. While we was waiting for the School doors to open we used to plan where we'd go. I got taken up for thieving coals. But they did reading. I never went back when I come out of prison.

Frederick
(Aged 12-14)

Jump For Your Life
Ken Whitmore

First presented by the Unicorn Theatre For Young People at the Arts Theatre, London in 1976.

FREDERICK has a difficult task – to persuade all of us in the world and in the audience, to jump into the air at a given moment, or the world will crash to pieces. He has received this startling information from a mole – who points out that the surface of this overcrowded globe is only held firm by the noble effort of the moles. But this is no longer enough – we must act now before it is too late.

In this opening scene set in a crowded Drill Hall, FREDERICK is pushed on to the stage. He is very nervous – in fact he would be speechless, if the situation of the world were not even more desperate than his shyness. Slowly he gathers confidence despite continued heckling from a disbelieving audience.

Published by Samuel French, London

FREDERICK

(*Into the wings*) All right! No need to shove. (*He takes four steps across the stage and stops when he sees the size of the audience. He is momentarily at a loss for words but falls back on his usual greeting*) Hello! How do? (*Pause*) By gumbo, hundreds of 'em! (*Pause*) Can you hear me all right? I'm a bit scared. I didn't expect so many of you. (*He scans the audience from side to side, up and down*) Hundreds of 'em! Hundreds of people who don't believe in the moles. Boys and girls, most of you. Some grown-ups a' course. I'm not surprised they don't believe. But boys and girls. I thought they could work things out – like – more clear. They've sent me here to change your minds for you. The Professor and Mr Harridge and Old Gumbolt. There's a load of people down at the Drill Hall who don't believe in the moles and won't jump at jumping time. That's what they said. Well, it's true. You can bet your life on that. It's true about the moles . . . It is! And if you don't all jump in the air two hours from now the whole world's going to be splintered to bits and we'll all be goners . . . You've *got* to believe. You've *got* to jump. Or we'll all go up in smoke. (*Pause*) Listen – you children. (*Pointing to the Hecklers*) Never mind what they say – Laurel and Hardy. At five o'clock tonight we've all got to jump in the air. All at the same time. You and me and everybody in every country and every island and every nation. Everybody. Chinese, Russians, English, Eskimoes – cannibals! All the folk in the world have got to be off the ground at the same split second. So there's not one foot touching the earth anywhere on this planet. Listen, all the grandmas and grandads are going to jump . . . I've got a letter here. (*He takes a letter from his pocket and holds it up*) Mrs Olga Shipoochin, aged ninety-seven, of Moscow. In Russia, that is. You should see all the letters I get. Tons! Now listen to this. (*He reads from the letter*) 'Dear Frederick Kitchener Spudkins,' – that's me – 'We will be thinking of you and jumping with you when the time comes. And my husband Nikolai, who only has one left leg . . . will be jumping as well. All best love, dear comrade jumper.' . . . And there's loads more I could tell you about but there's not the time. There's only two hours left. (*He glances at his watch*) One hour and forty-eight minutes . . . O.K. Tell me this, then. Even if you're right. Even if the moles can't save the world. Even if nothing horrible is going to happen and it's all a – a fantastic fib. What have you got to lose by standing up and giving a little jump, eh? Like this. (*He jumps*) Look. How's it going to spoil your day just to give a little jump? (*He jumps*) Like that.

William

Just William
'William and the Russian Prince'
Richmal Crompton

Originally written in 1922 and shown on BBC Television in 1994. Young WILLIAM BROWN's brother Robert has received an invitation to the cricket week at Marleigh Manor – a most important social event. WILLIAM has offered to go with him as his valet or butler, but Robert threatens that if he comes near the place he will wring his neck. When a day has passed and there is no news of Robert, WILLIAM's curiosity gets the better of him and he sets off for Marleigh Manor. Everyone there is out in the grounds watching the cricket. WILLIAM creeps along in a ditch at the far end of the field and sees Robert sitting on a bench, looking forlorn. Next to him is a beautiful blonde girl in deep conversation with a tall, dark young man. They are both ignoring Robert. Determined to help his brother, WILLIAM devises a plan.

In this scene the blonde girl is walking down the field towards the woods. She hears a loud cough and turns to see WILLIAM crouching behind a bush. She demands haughtily to know what he is doing there.

Published by Macmillan Children's Books, London

WILLIAM

I'm on guard . . . There's a Russian prince playin' cricket with those
people an' I've been told by Scotland Yard to guard him . . . You see,
they thought that no one would think it funny to see a boy hanging
round watching a cricket match, but a policeman or plain-clothes
man would make people sort of suspicious. I'm a good deal older
than what I look, of course. I've been kept small by Scotland Yard
so as to be able to take on jobs like this. Anyway, I'm supposed to
be watchin' this Russian prince to see no harm comes to him . . .
(WILLIAM *looks over to where the game is going on*) It's that one . . . the
one batting now . . . He was rescued from the revolution when he
was a boy and brought over here secret and given to this family to
pretend he was their son so as to keep him in hiding. You see,
(WILLIAM's *voice sinks to a sinister whisp*er) you see the Bolshevists are
after him. He got away with all his jewels for one thing, and they're
after his jewels. You see that very dark man over there? . . . Well,
he's a Bolshevist. He's after the jewels. That's why I'm told to guard
this Russian prince against him . . . (*He assumes a mysterious
expression*) Oh, I've got ways. I've got secret signals. I could have all
Scotland Yard here in no time if I gave some of my secret signals . . .
You won't tell anyone, will you? (*Anxiously*) I mean – well, they'd
probably get him at once if they knew anyone knew . . . You see, (*he
hisses*) your life'll be in danger too if anyone finds out you know . . .
And most of all you mustn't let him know you know . . . If the
prince knew you knew he'd go straight away an' none of us would
ever see him again.

Jay
(A bird)

The See-Saw Tree

David Wood

First performed at the Redgrave Theatre, Farnham in 1986 by the
Farnham Repertory Company. The play looks at the world of an
oak tree – the See-Saw Tree – and the animals dwelling in and
around it, whose lives are shattered by the news that the tree is
about to be felled.

In this early scene the Mistlethrush is singing loudly and out of
tune – a dreadful noise – when suddenly JAY arrives. He is brashly
confident, a salesbird supreme. Inside his coat his 'wares' are neatly
displayed – dried grasses, quality mosses and badger hair. He
carries a suitcase filled with special cleaning materials all ready to
sell to his reluctant neighbours – Mistlethrush, Dunnock and
Squirrel. He lands on a branch just below Mistlethrush and near to
Squirrel's drey.

Published by Amber Lane Press, Charlbury, Oxfordshire

JAY

What music fills my ears? . . . Such tone. Such pitch. Such artistry
. . . Jay's the name, madam. Travelling salesbird supreme . . . I have
been on a flight of exploration, madam, spreading my wings far
and wide in search of marketable merchandise. Scouring the
countryside for new and exciting lines to offer my lucky customers
at bargain prices. What do you fancy? . . . Aha! See my selection,
perfect for the use of building nests. (*He opens his coat. Inside his
wares are neatly displayed*) Dried grasses, bracken, quality mosses,
badger hair, sheep's wool for extra warmth, polythene and paper.
Pick your own, mix 'n' match, yours for the modest sum of two
acorns. Can't say fairer than that . . . Do me a favour . . . Aha! Think
ahead, madam. Think of when your eggs hatch. Think of all those
hungry little beaks to feed. No problem. (*He opens the other side of his
coat, revealing more merchandise*) I've got crab apples, juicy slugs,
calorie-stuffed caterpillars, mouthwatering worms, specially
selected spiders, meaty maggots and crunchy moths. Take your
pick . . . Your loss, dear lady, not mine. Happy laying . . . (*He
approaches Squirrel's drey*) Wakey, wakey! Anyone at home?
(*Dunnock appears, carrying rubbish from the drey*) Give a bird a
chance, Dunnock! Where's Squirrel? . . . Cleaning? Aha! Glad you
said that. Ideal for the use of. (*He opens his 'suitcase', displaying more
wares*) Look at this little lot. Bark scourer, lichen loosener, fungus
flusher, mildew stripper, leafmould remover. Tried and tested.
Satisfaction guaranteed . . . I'm only asking one acorn per item.

Eleonora

Easter

August Strindberg
Translated by Peter Watts

First performed at the Intima Teatern, Stockholm in 1901 and set in the small provincial town of Lund over Easter.

ELEONORA is a young, sensitive girl who has just returned from the Asylum where she was being treated for a mental breakdown. She has broken into a flower shop which was closed for Confirmation Day, and has taken a daffodil in a pot as a present for her brother – leaving her card and a kroner on the counter. Her father is serving a prison sentence for embezzlement and the family are haunted by creditors. The chief of these is the sinister Lindkurst, who walks past the house each day, but so far has never knocked on the door.

It is Good Friday, and in this scene ELEONORA is talking to Benjamin, a young schoolboy who is being tutored by her brother. She starts up when a police whistle is heard, as she is afraid of being arrested for taking the daffodil, but it is only boys playing in the street. She tortures herself with the thought that Lindkurst may appear at any moment and take away the furniture.

Published by Penguin Classics, London

ELEONORA

Let him come! Then we shall have to go. We must leave everything
– all the old furniture that Father got together for us, and that I've
known ever since I was a child. Yes, we oughtn't to own anything
that binds us to this earth . . . Do you know what I shall find it
hardest to part from? That clock over there; it was there when I was
born, and it's measured out all the hours and days for me ever
since. (*She lifts the clock from the table*) Can you hear – it's like a heart
beating – just like a heart. And it stopped at the very moment my
grandfather died – yes, we had it even then! Good-bye, little clock
– soon you'll stop again. Do you know, when there was no luck in
the house, it used to go fast – just as if it wanted to get the bad times
over quickly – for *us*, of course. But when times were happy, it used
to go slow, so that we could enjoy them longer. It was a kind clock.
But there was an unkind one, too – that's why it has to hang in the
kitchen now. It couldn't bear music, because as soon as Elis played
the piano, it began to strike. We all noticed it, not just me. That's
why it has to stay in the kitchen, because it was wicked. But Lina
doesn't like it either, because it's noisy at night, and she can't boil
eggs by it – they always turn out hard-boiled, Lina says. Now
you're laughing! . . . It's clearing up outside already, and there's fine
weather coming; the snow is melting, you can smell the thaw even
in here, and tomorrow the violets will be out along the south wall.
The clouds have lifted, I know they have, because I can breathe
again. Oh, I know so well when the Heavens are open. Go and open
the curtains, Benjamin. I want God to see us! (*Benjamin gets up and
does so; the moonlight streams into the room*) Look! the full moon! It's
the Easter moon, and now, although it's the moon that's shining,
you know that the sun is still there.

Tulip
(Aged 15)

Eclipse

Simon Armitage

Commissioned for *Connections 97* by the Royal National Theatre, this is a poetic drama set in Cornwall in 1999. An unseen group of adults gather on the headland to watch the eclipse of the sun, while their teenaged offspring – TULIP, Klondile, Midnight, Glue Boy, Polly and Jane – are on the beach below. A strange girl, Lucy appears to challenge each and every one of the young people and then vanishes. The action of the play alternates between the beach and the police station, where they try to make sense of and come to terms with Lucy's disappearance.

This scene is set in the police Interview Room, where TULIP, a tomboy wearing Dr Marten boots and a red headscarf tied like a pirate, gives her version of the events.

From: *New Connections – New Plays for Young People*
Published by Faber & Faber, London

TULIP

When she left us for good I was nine or ten.
Ran off with the milkman, so Dad said. Ran off
with the man in the moon, as far as I care.
Grew up with uncles, cousins, played rugby-football,
swapped a pram for a ten-speed drop-handlebar,
played with matches instead, flags and cars, threw
the dolls on a skip and the skates on a dustcart,
flogged the frills and pink stuff at a car-boot sale,
burnt the Girl Guide outfit in the back garden,
got kitted out at Famous Army Stores and Top Man.
And Oxfam. I'll tell you something that sums it up:
found a doll's-house going mouldy in the attic –
boarded it up, kept a brown rat in it.
Put it all behind now, growing out of it, Dad says, says
I'm blossoming, and I suppose he must be right. Klondike?
No, not a boyfriend, more like a kid brother, really,
known him since as far back as I can remember.
Kissed him? Who wants to know? I mean no, Sir,
except on his head, just once, on his birthday.
Him and Lucy? Well, she took a shine to him,
he told her some things and I think she liked him.
She just showed up and wanted to tag along,
make some friends, I suppose, mess about, have fun;
she had a few tricks up her sleeve, wanted . . . all right,
if you put it like that . . . to be one of the group.
It's not much cop being on your own. Which was fine
by us. It's not that we gave it a second thought
to tell you the truth. She just turned up that afternoon
like a lost dog. She was one of the gang. Then she was
gone.

Nazreen
(South Asian)

In the Sweat

Naomi Wallace and Bruce McLeod

This is one of the plays for young people commissioned for *New Connections* and performed on the Cottesloe and Olivier stages of the Royal National Theatre in 1997.

The action takes place in a disused Synagogue in Spitalfields, London – an area noted for its nonconformity. Four young people – Fitch, an Afro-Caribbean boy; Scudder, a homeless white boy; Duncan, a twenty-one year old security guard; and NAZREEN, a South Asian girl – are thrown together. The play deals with extreme situation. As their violent confrontation begins to reveal their ties to one another, an elderly Sephardic Jew, Antonio, appears dragging a stone.

Towards the end of the play, NAZREEN recounts the horrific story of her elder sister, traumatised when racists petrol-bombed the phone booth she was in.

From: *New Connections – New Plays for Young People*
Published by Faber & Faber, London

NAZREEN

Seven years ago. Yes. Like. Seven hundred. My sister, Mahfuza, and I, we went out to use the phone. To call for flowers. It was my mother's birthday and her favourites were – they were – yes. Mimosa. Small yellow flowers, thin stalks. Mimosa. They smell like dust. Almost sweet. I waited on the corner to make sure my mother did not see us making the call as she walked home from work. Mahfuza was older than me but smaller and had to stand on her toes to put the coins in and dial the number. And then suddenly they were there, three of them, tall, fast boys, who moved quick, quick. Like white flames they sprung up from the stone of the pavement. (*NAZREEN steps on to the old stone*) One of them had a can and he circled the phone booth, wetting it like a dog. Another wedged something against the door so my sister could not get out. The third boy, I remember he was laughing but his laugh was strange, almost like crying. He lay broken pieces of wood against the door of the booth and lit the match. And suddenly it seemed the glass of the phone booth started to burn. My sister still had the receiver to her ear, but she was no longer speaking. Her mouth was open. So open. But no sound. And I had started to run towards her. But by then the flames were high and someone grabbed me and held me back. And Mahfuza's mouth was still open behind the flames, as though she were going to eat them. As though she could swallow them whole. And there was smoke, lots of it, and after some moments I could only see the top of Mahfuza's head in the booth, her black hair blacker than the smoke.

The neighbours got her out. In time. What does that mean? In time? In time for what? For months and months after I came home from school I sat with Mahfuza by the window. I wondered if she was looking out for the three young men. Afraid they might come back. But the expression on her face was not one of fear. It was not one of anything. And no matter how many times we bathed her, for years afterwards, her hair still smelled of smoke. It wouldn't wash out. There's nothing wrong with her body but she doesn't walk. There's nothing wrong with her mouth but she doesn't speak. I look at her and I think: 'She is my England.' No, I say. But the hands in her lap, they are cold. 'She is my England.' I say no. Not for me . . . For Mahfuza. Perhaps. Yes, for Mahfuza, that silence. Sometimes that's how it happens. But not for me. No, not that for me.

Lisa
(London, aged 17)

The Power of the Dog

Ellen Dryden

First performed at The Orange Tree Theatre, Richmond in 1996.

Vivien Chadwick, Head of the English Department in a failing school run by an incompetent Headmaster, is preparing to take up a new appointment as Head of a school in South London. At the same time she is attempting to move house as well as visit her mother who has had a stroke,

Added to these problems is LISA, a brilliant but difficult sixth former, who she is encouraging to stay on at school and try for a place in university. In this scene Vivien is in her study waiting for LISA to arrive for an extra tutorial. LISA turns up late as usual with the same old excuses – waiting thirty-five minutes for the bus and Mum being stroppy. Vivien asks if there is any chance of Mum coming to see her

Published by First Writes Publications, London

LISA

Nah! She doesn't like schools. Give her panic attacks. (*Pause*) And I don't want you to come to my house . . . (*LISA turns her back. Then changes the subject with great energy*) Listen. I reckon you owe me ten quid. I went to see that *Midsummer Night's Dream*. It was rubbish! Helena was about thirty-five, kept chucking herself all over the place – tossing her hair back and flinging her arms about. You know – just like young people always do when we're in love. Nearly ruptured herself. She was about six inches shorter than Hermia as well, so she'd got these gross high heels and Hermia had to bend at the knees all through the quarrel scene. And the Mechanicals wandered about in the audience and talked to us. I hate that! And Peter Quince sat in the Stalls and shouted his lines from there. And the fairies all lived in cardboard boxes and had tattoos. Puck was a drug-pusher. And it went on for nearly four hours. I reckon ours was better. And I couldn't afford it! . . .

Hey and guess what! Theseus and Hypolita played Oberon and Titania! Isn't that original? Everybody liked it except me. I wanted to get up and kill them all. Bunch of no-hopers . . . I really love that play . . . I don't think this had any . . . respect. And it wasn't – magic . . . (*She stops, lost in thought for a moment*) I know. 'The best in this kind are but shadows and the worst no worse if imagination amend them . . . It must be your imagination then and not theirs.' (*She is very still. Her face becomes a mask*)

(*Very quietly*) I like – magic. (*Briskly*) I suppose I'm talking rubbish – everybody else says it's brilliant. And they're paid to be in the imagination business, aren't they? And I've got no right to criticize them.

Martha
(Yorkshire)

The Secret Garden

Frances Hodgson Burnett
Adapted for the theatre by Thérèse Kitchin

First performed at the Farrer Theatre, Eton in 1990 and then at the Wilde Theatre in 1995 by the Quercus Theatre Company. The action takes place in 1911.

Young Mary Lennox has been sent from India to live in her uncle's big house in Yorkshire. Her uncle, a strange withdrawn man, wants nothing to do with her and leaves her in the charge of his stern housekeeper, Mrs Medlock and MARTHA – a young servant girl. MARTHA is sorry for Mary and does her best to cheer her up. She encourages her to play out in the grounds, and it is here that Mary finds an old walled garden that has been locked up for years. She asks the gardener about it, and is told not to 'poke her nose where it's no cause to go'.

In this scene she begs MARTHA to tell her the story of the secret garden and reluctantly MARTHA explains that it had once belonged to her uncle's young wife who died ten years ago.

Published by William Heinemann Ltd, Oxford

MARTHA

Mrs Medlock says it's not to be talked about. Mrs Medlock says his troubles are nowt of his servants' business. Tha'lt get me into trouble . . . I'll lose my place here, then what'll mother do . . . If it weren't for garden – he wouldn't be as he is . . . She made it her own – none of t'gardeners was ever let in . . . Him an' her they looked after it themselves . . . They'd shut t'door an' stay there for hours – laughin' an' talkin' . . . as though it were a world of their own . . . They planted roses – wild, climbin' things – He built her a swing – an' she fashioned a seat in t'branch of old tree . . . Even now I want to cry . . . The bough broke an' she fell to the ground . . . Mother says she was just a slip of a thing most likely teasin' him from up there in the tree . . . She was hurt so bad that soon after she died . . . If she hadn't been as she was – she might have got better . . . There's lots of things that are not to be talked of in this place . . . Anyway – that's what happened and he nearly went mad an' he's never recovered . . . You musn't tell Mrs Medlock what I've told you . . . Promise . . . An' now tha'lt be a good child an' not try to wander where tha's not meant to go. Tha's better off than some. Mother says you ought to be learnin' thy books, an' tha 'ought to have a woman to look after you. Mother says, 'You just think how you'd feel, Martha, shut up by thee sen in a big place like that with no other . . . You do your best to cheer her up.' So I brought thee a present . . . (*Holds out skipping rope*) What is it for! Does tha' mean they've got no skippin' ropes in India for all they've got elephants and tigers. This is what it's for . . . (*She skips . . . stopping*) I could skip longer than that. I've skipped as much as five hundred when I was twelve – you have a try . . . It'll tire you out, then you'll sleep an' not bother about wind howling!

The Grand High Witch

The Witches

Roald Dahl
Adapted by David Wood

First performed at the Lyceum Theatre, Sheffield in 1992 and then at the Duke of York's Theatre, London.

The Witches are holding their annual meeting at the Hotel Magnificent, Bournemouth, under the cover name of The Royal Society of the Prevention of Cruelty to Children. The meeting is presided over by the GRAND HIGH WITCH, who having removed her wig and mask – revealing a wizened, horrible, rotting face – proceeds to lay out her plan to 'rub out' all the children of England within a year.

Published by Samuel French, London

GRAND HIGH WITCH

You may rrree-moof your vigs, and get some fresh air into your spotty scalps. (*The Witches reveal their bald heads*) Vitches of Inkland. Miserrrable vitches. Useless lazy vitches. You are a heap of idle good-for-nothing vurms! . . . As I am eating my lunch, I am looking out of the vindow at the beach. And vot am I seeing? I am seeing a rrrevolting sight, which is putting me off my food. Hundreds of rrrotten rrrepulsive children. Playing on the sand. Vye have you not got rrrid of them? Vye? . . . You vill do better . . . My orders are that every single child in Inkland shall be rrrubbed out, sqvashed, sqvirted, sqvittered and frittered before I come here again in vun year's time . . . Who said that? Who dares to argue with me? (*She points dramatically at Witch Two*) It vos you, vos it not? . . . Come here. (*She beckons. Witch Two, mesmerised, ascends the platform*)

> A vitch who dares to say I'm wrrrong
> Vill not be vith us very long!
>
> A stupid vitch who answers back
> Must burn until her bones are black!

(*Staring at Witch Two, the GRAND HIGH WITCH gestures. Sparks fly. Smoke rises – Witch Two disappears*) I hope nobody else is going to make me cross today. (*She finds the smouldering remnants of Witch Two's clothes and holds them up*) Frrrizzled like a frrritter. Cooked like a carrot. You vill never see her again. Now vee can get down to business . . . I am having a plan. A giganticus plan! . . . You vill buy sveetshops . . . You vill fill them high with luscious sveets and tasty chocs! . . . You vill have a Great Gala Opening with free sveets and chocs for every child! . . . You vill be filling every choc and every sveet with my latest and grrreatest magic formula. (*She produces a potion bottle*) Formula Eighty-Six Delayed Action Mouse-Maker! . . . To cause delayed action, rrroast in the oven vun alarm-clock set to go off at nine o'clock in the morning . . . Inject vun droplet of the formula in each sveet or choc, open your shop, and as the children pour in on their vay home from school . . . (*she chants*)

> Crrram them full of sticky eats,
> Send them home still guzzling sveets,
> And in the morning little fools
> Go marching off to separate schools.

Ronnie

Chicken Soup with Barley
Arnold Wesker

First produced at the Belgrade Theatre, Coventry in 1958 and later transferred to the Royal Court Theatre in London. Part of *The Wesker Trilogy*, this is the story of an East End family and their gradual disillusionment as one by one their ideals slip away from them. The early part of the play covers the period before the Second World War, with the excitement over the Spanish Civil War of the thirties and the anti-Blackshirt demonstrations. Then, later, we see the characters devoting their energies towards the creation of a new world.

In this scene it is October 1947. RONNIE, now a teenager, is listening to the wireless and conducting an imaginary orchestra, when his Aunt Cissie lets herself into the house. She asks him if his father is still working in the same job.

Published by Samuel French, London

RONNIE

No, he's a store-keeper in a sweet factory now. Look. (*Shows her a biscuit tin full of sweets*) Jelly babies. Can't help himself. Doesn't do it on a large scale, mind, just a handful each night. Everyone does it . . . You know he can't stay long at a job – and now he has got what he has always wanted – a legitimate excuse . . . He walks – slowly and stooped – with his head sunk into his shoulders, hands in his pockets (*imitates his father*). His step isn't sure – frightened to exert himself in case he should suddenly drop dead. You ought to see him in a strong wind – (*moves drunkenly round the room*) – like an autumn leaf. He seems to have given up the fight, as though *thank God* he was no longer responsible for himself. You know, Aunt, I don't suppose there is anything more terrifying to a man than his own sense of failure, and your brother Harry is really a very sensitive man. No one knows more than he does how he's failed. Now that's tragedy for you: having the ability to see what is happening to yourself and yet not being able to do anything about it. Like a long nightmare. God! fancy being born just to live a long nightmare. He gets around. But who knows how sick he is? Now we can't tell his lethargy from his illness . . . Here! (*Goes to a drawer and takes out a notebook*) Did you know he once started to write his autobiography? Listen. (*Reads*) 'Of me, the dummy and my family.' How's that for a poetic title! 'Sitting at my work in the shop one day my attention was drawn to the dummy that we all try the work on. The rhythm of the machines and my constant looking at the dummy rocked me off in a kind of sleepy daze. And to my surprise the dummy began to take the shape of a human, it began to speak. Softly at first, so softly I could hardly hear it. And then louder and still louder, and it seemed to raise its eyebrows and with a challenge asked: your life, what of your life? My life? I had never thought, and I began to take my mind back, way back to the time when I was a little boy.' There, a whole notebook full, and then one day he stopped! Just like that! God knows why a man stops doing the one thing that can keep him together.

Loll
(Gloucestershire)

Cider with Rosie

Laurie Lee

A Stage Adaptation by James Roose-Evans

Performed at the Hampstead Theatre in 1963 and later transferred to the Garrick Theatre, London. The poet, Laurie Lee – known as LOLL to his family and friends – looks back on scenes from his childhood in a Cotswold village.

In this scene he remembers a family picnic, with his mother, the children from her husband's first marriage, Marge, Doth and Phyll and his two brothers, Jack and Tony. Phyll asks their mother to tell them about their uncles. LOLL reminds them of Uncle Sid and the time he got the sack from the bus company.

(*Note* In the play the Narrator, Laurie Lee, is played by an adult actor remembering his childhood self. The young Laurie Lee – known as LOLL to his family – is played by a young actor. However, for the purpose of this extract I have joined their two speeches together. Also note the characters were originally played in Gloucestershire accents – but as an audition speech this is a matter of individual choice.)

Published by Samuel French, London

LOLL

Our Uncle Sid was the best double-decker bus driver in Stroud, without doubt, even safer, more inspired when he drank. Everbody knew this, except the bus company. He began to get lectures, admonitions, stern warnings, and finally suspensions without pay. When this last happened, out of respect for our Aunt Alice, he always committed suicide. Indeed, he committed suicide more than any man I know. But always in the most reasonable manner. If he drowned himself, then the canal was dry. If he jumped down a well, so was that; and when he drank disinfectant there was always an antidote ready, clearly marked, to save everyone the trouble. He reasoned, quite rightly, that Aunt Alice's anger, on hearing of another suspension, would be swallowed by her larger anxiety on finding him again so near to death. And Auntie Alice never failed him in this and forgave him each time he recovered. The bus company were almost equally forgiving, they took him back again and again. Mam, do you remember the time when the bus company gave Uncle Sid the sack for good? . . . They found him asleep at the wheel – he were drunk! And that night, we were sitting by the fire when there was a knock at the door. It were Auntie Alice and the girls. They were all dressed in black. 'He's done it this time,' she said, 'He's gone off to end it all. He's gone to Deadcombe Wood. He always told me he would!' And then she turned to our Mam and said, 'Oh, Nance, Nance, he'll do himself in. Your boys, they just got to find him.' So Jack and I put on our coats and we went up the valley, towards Deadcombe Wood. It were raining. We beat up and down through the wood, calling 'Uncle, Uncle!' We were real scared. We didn't know what we might find. We were about to go home when suddenly we saw him. He were standing on tiptoe under an oak tree with his braces round his neck, looped to a branch. The elastic made him bob up and down! He were in a terrible temper. Do you know what he said? *'You've been a bloody long time!'*

Midnight
(Teenager)

Eclipse
Simon Armitage

Commissioned for *Connections 97* by the Royal National Theatre, this is a poetic drama set in Cornwall in 1999. An unseen group of adults gather on the headland to watch the eclipse of the sun, while their teenaged offspring – MIDNIGHT, Tulip, Klondike, Glue Boy and Polly and Jane – are on the beach below. A strange girl, Lucy appears to challenge each and every one of the young people and then vanishes. The action of the play alternates between the beach and the police station, where they try to make sense of and come to terms with Lucy's disappearance.

This scene is set in the police Interview Room, where MIDNIGHT, a blind boy, is the first to make his statement.

From: *New Connections – New Plays for Young People*
Published by Faber & Faber, London

MIDNIGHT

(*A police interview room*) Martin Blackwood, they call me Midnight –
it's a sick joke but I don't mind. Coffee
please, two sugars, white – don't ask me
to say that I saw, I'm profoundly blind,
but I'll tell you as much as I can, all right?

Cornwall, August, as you know. There's a beach
down there, seaside and all that, cliffs with caves
at the back, but up on the hill there's a view
looking south, perfect for watching a total eclipse
of the sun. The mums and dads were up on the top,
we were down in the drop – we'd just gone along
for the trip, killing a few hours. You see
it's like watching birds or trains, but with planets
and stars, and about as much fun as cricket
in my condition, or 3D. There was Glue Boy,
Polly and Jane, Tulip and Klondike and me.
Thing is, we were messing around in the caverns
when Lucy appeared. Her mother and father
were up with the rest of the spotters; she wasn't
from round here. Thing is, I was different then,
did a lot of praying, wore a cross, went to church,
thought I was walking towards the light of the Lord –
when it's as dark as it is in here, you follow
any road with any torch. Lucy put me on the straight
and narrow. There's no such thing as the soul,
there's bone and there's marrow. It's just biology.
You make your own light, follow your own nose.
She came and she went. And that's as much as I know.

Scudder
(Aged 16)

In the Sweat

Naomi Wallace and Bruce McLeod

This is one of the plays for young people commissioned for *New Connections* and performed on the Cottesloe and Olivier stages of the Royal National Theatre in 1997.

The action takes place in a disused Synagogue in Spitalfields, London – an area noted for its nonconformity, where Fitch, an Afro-Caribbean boy, Nazreen, a South Asian girl, Duncan, a security guard and SCUDDER, a homeless white boy are thrown together. The play deals with extreme situation. As their violent confrontation begins to reveal their ties to one another, an elderly Sephardic Jew, Antonio, appears dragging a stone.

In this opening scene, SCUDDER enters, performing slow and controlled cartwheels as he circles the lone figure of Duncan, seated and covered with a blanket.

From: *New Connections – New Plays for Young People*
Published by Faber & Faber, London

SCUDDER

Princelet, Fournier, Wilkes, Fashion. Hanbury, Lamb, Heneage, Chicksand. (*He pauses in his cartwheeling*) This is my place. You gotta draw a line somewhere. (*He begins cartwheels again*) Fleur de Lis, Folgate, Elder, Calvin. Quaker, Deal, Woodseer, Buxton. It's not my 'patch', my bit of 'turf'. It's my ways and means. Commercial, Wentworth, Brune, Hunton. Streets are fine, but it's the lanes that count: Artillery, Brick, Bell and Petticoat. (*Duncan moans. SCUDDER falls to a sitting position*) You're awake then. (*Duncan makes another sound*) Sorry. (*Beat*) Princelet, Fournier . . . (*He begins cartwheels again*) Wilkes, Fashion. I know my way around. Got a brick cross my skull on Osborn. Dropped it from my list right then and there. You can't keep a street that's turned against you. (*He comes to a halt*) Broke my heart to lose it. (*Beat*) Princelet, Fournier. But it's how I know what's what, who I've got, who I got to get to know, and who hates me. You hate me. (*SCUDDER hears a noise. Duncan grunts. SCUDDER slaps Duncan's head to shush him, stuffs some more of the blanket into Duncan's mouth*) Shut it . . . (*Fitch and Nazreen enter. They are wearing school uniforms. They do not immediately see Duncan. SCUDDER comes forward. He is both nervous and overly excited*) A room of one's own. No view to speak of. Just me . . . I've been here a month and not a rabbi in sight. There've been some weird noises though. Might be haunted . . . Berwards Lane? (*He does a slow cartwheel as he repeats the word 'Berwards'. Then he stops abruptly*) Nope . . . Look. An orange is an orange, right? A thumb has got two bones. One, two. Easy. Berwards isn't a street. Fact. You must have read it wrong . . . I don't just know the names. I make the streets. Happen. What I walk, I make. You know, mark them, make sure they run on time, then double back and change direction before the light turns red. But I like crossing over best. Unpredictable. You cross a street like you cross a man's mind, without warning, and if you're good you leave no tracks behind. Right? And Spitalfields. It's *my* domain.

Hally
(South African)

'Master Harold' . . . and the Boys
Athol Fugard

Performed at the Market Theatre, Johannesburg in 1983 and later
that year at the National Theatre in London, the play opens in the
St George's Park Tea Room on a wet and windy Port Elizabeth
afternoon in 1950. HALLY, a young white South African boy, son of
the tea-room proprietess has just got back from school. Sam, a black
waiter in his forties, fetches a towel for him to dry his hair. HALLY
has always been closer to Sam than to his own parents, and in this
scene HALLY remembers the time Sam made a kite for him.

From: *Athol Fugard – Selected Plays*, published by Oxford Paperbacks, Oxford

HALLY

It started off looking like another of those useless nothing-to-do afternoons. I'd already been down to Main Street looking for adventure, but nothing had happened. I didn't feel like climbing trees in the Donkin Park or pretending I was a private eye and following a stranger . . . so as usual: See what's cooking in Sam's room. This time it was you on the floor. You had two thin pieces of wood and you were smoothing them down with a knife. It didn't look particularly interesting, but when I asked you what you were doing, you just said, 'Wait and see, Hally. Wait . . . and see' . . . in that secret sort of way of yours, so I knew there was a surprise coming. You teased me, you bugger, by being deliberately slow and not answering my questions! (*Sam laughs*) And whistling while you worked away! God, it was infuriating! I could have brained you! It was only when you tied them together in a cross and put that down on the brown paper that I realised what you were doing. 'Sam is making a kite?' And when I asked you and you said 'Yes' . . . (*Shaking his head with disbelief*) The sheer audacity of it took my breath away. I mean, seriously, what the hell does a black man know about flying a kite? . . . When we left the boarding house to go up onto the hill, I was praying quietly that there wouldn't be any other kids around to laugh at us . . . Can you remember what the poor thing looked like? Tomato-box wood and brown paper! Flour and water for glue! Two of my mother's old stockings for a tail, and then all those bits and pieces of string you made me tie together so that we could fly it! . . . You went a little distance from me down the hill, you held it up ready to let it go . . . 'That is it,' I thought. 'like everything else in my life, here comes another fiasco.' Then you shouted, 'Go, Hally!' and I started to run. (*Another pause*) I don't know how to describe it, Sam. *Ja!* The miracle happened! I was running, waiting for it to crash to the ground, but instead suddenly there was something alive behind me at the end of the string, tugging at it as if it wanted to be free. I looked back . . .(*Shakes his head*) . . . I still can't believe my eyes. It was flying! . . . It was sort of sad bringing it down, Sam. And it looked sad again when it was lying there on the ground. Like something that had lost its soul. Just tomato-box wood, brown paper and two of my mother's old stockings! But, hell, I'll never forget that first moment when I saw it up there. I had a stiff neck the next day from looking up so much.

The Artful Dodger

Oliver Twist

Charles Dickens

Written in 1838, this is the story of a young orphan, Oliver, who runs away to London and meets up with another boy, Jack Dawkins, known as the ARTFUL DODGER. The DODGER introduces Oliver to the sinister Fagin, who runs a Thieves Den, sending out young boys to pick the pockets of the rich.

In this scene, Oliver is on his knees cleaning the DODGER's boots for him, while DODGER explains the advantages of joining Fagin's gang. Although the DODGER is young and only four foot six tall, he has all the airs and manners of a man about town.

DODGER

(*Sighs and resumes his pipe*) I suppose you don't even know what a prig is? . . . I am. I'd scorn to be anything else. So's Charley. So's Fagin. So's Sikes. So's Nancy. So's Bet. So we all are, down to the dog. And he's the downiest one of the lot! He wouldn't so much as bark in a witness-box for fear of committing himself; no, not if you tied him up in one, and left him there without wittles for a fortnight. He's a rum dog. Don't he look fierce at any strange cove that laughs or sings when he's in company! Won't he growl at all, when he hears a fiddle playing! And don't he hate other dogs as ain't of his breed! – Oh no! He's an out-and-out Christian . . . Why don't you put yourself under Fagin, Oliver? And make a fortun' out of hand? And so be able to retire on your property, and do the gen-teel; as I mean to, in the very next leap-year but four that ever comes, and the forty-second Tuesday in Trinity-week . . . Go! Why, where's your spirit? Don't you take any pride out of yourself? Would you go and be dependent on your friends ? . . . Look here. (*Drawing forth a handful of shillings and halfpence*) Here's a jolly life! What's the odds where it comes from? Here, catch hold; there's plenty more where they were took from . . . You've been brought up bad. Fagin will make something of you, though, or you'll be the first he ever had that turned out unprofitable. You'd better begin at once; for you'll come to the trade long before you think of it; and you're only losing time, Oliver . . . If you don't take pocket-handkerchers and watches, some other cove will; so that the coves that lose 'em will be the worse, and you'll be all the worse too, and nobody half a ha'p'orth the better, except the chaps wot gets them – and you've just as good a right to them as they have.

Ronnie Winslow
(Aged 14)

The Winslow boy

Terence Rattigan

First produced in London in 1946, where it won an award for best play of the year, was made into a film, and then was filmed again in 1999 and directed by American playwright David Mamet. It is set in Arthur Winslow's house in Kensington, London just before the 1914–18 war and is based on the true story of a father's fight to clear his son of theft.

Fourteen-year-old cadet RONNIE WINSLOW has been expelled from the Royal Naval College, Osborne for the theft of a five-shilling postal order. All appeals to the college and the Lords of the Admiralty are in vain. In a final attempt to clear his son's name, Arthur Winslow has now called in the best advocate in England, Sir Robert Morton, to take over his son's case.

In this scene, set in the Winslow's drawing room, RONNIE is standing at the table facing Sir Robert. He is looking very spick and span in his Eton suit. His father and sister are also in the room. Sir Robert asks RONNIE to recount in his own words, the events leading up to his accusation.

Published by Samuel French, London

RONNIE

Well, it was a half-holiday, so we didn't have any work after dinner
. . . [*Sir Robert: Dinner?*] Yes. At one o'clock. Until prep. at seven . . .
Just before dinner I went to the Chief Petty Officer and asked him
to let me have fifteen and six out of what I had in the College Bank
. . . I wanted to buy an air-pistol . . . I had dinner . . . Then I went to
the locker-room and put the fifteen and six in my locker . . . I went
to get permission to go down to the post office. Then I went to the
locker-room again, got out my money, and went down to the post
office . . . I bought my postal order . . . Then I went back to college.
Then I met Elliot minor, and he said: 'I say, isn't it rot? Someone's
broken into my locker and pinched a postal order. I've reported it
to the P.O.' . . . He might have used another word for rot . . . Well
then, just before prep., I was told to go along and see Commander
Flower. The woman from the post office was there, and the
Commander said: 'Is this the boy?' and she said, 'It might be. I can't
be sure. They all look so much alike' . . . Then she said: 'I only know
that the boy who bought a postal order for fiteen and six was the
same boy that cashed one for five shillings.' So the Commander
said: 'Did you buy a postal order for fifteen and six?' And I said,
'Yes,' and then they made me write Elliot minor's name on an
envelope, and compared it to the signature on the postal order –
then they sent me to the sanatorium, and ten days later I was
sacked – I mean – expelled.

Useful Addresses

The Actors' Theatre School
32 Exeter Road
London   NW2 4SB
Tel: 020 8450 0371
Fax: 020 8450 1057

Offstage Theatre and Film Bookshop
37 Chalk Farm Road
London   NW1 8AJ
Tel: 020 7485 4996
Fax: 020 7916 8046

The British Library
96 Euston Road
London   NW1 2DB
Tel: 020 7412 7677 (*Reader Admissions*)

Victoria Library
160 Buckingham Palace Road
London   SW1W 9UD
Tel: 020 7641 4287

London Academy of Music and Dramatic Art (LAMDA)
Tower House
226 Cromwell Road
London   SW5 0SR
Tel: 020 7373 9883

Guildhall School of Music and Drama
Barbican
London   EC2Y 8DT
Tel: 020 7382 7167 (*Examinations Service*)

Copyright Holders

The following have granted permission for the reprinting of copyright material.

GIRLS 6-8

Have You Seen Zandile? by Gcina Mhlophe, Maralin Vanrenen and Thembi Mtshali. Reproduced by permission of Methuen Publishing Ltd. Published by Heinemann, USA and Methuen, UK.

The Lion, the Witch and the Wardrobe by C.S. Lewis, dramatised by Adrian Mitchell. Reproduced by permission of Oberon Books Ltd. Published by Oberon Books, London.

Extract from *The Magic Mirror* is reproduced by permission of Samuel French Ltd, 52 Fitzroy Street, London W1P 6JR to whom applications for public performance should be made.

The Mystery of the Pie and the Patty-Pan. Extract from *Mrs Tiggy-Winkle & Friends* dramatized by Rona Laurie. Copyright © Frederick Warne & Co., 1980. Reproduced by kind permission of Frederick Warne & Co. Published by Puffin Books, London.

Extract from *Tom Kitten and his Friends* by Adrian Mitchell. Copyright © Adrian Mitchell & Frederick Warne & Co., 1998. Reproduced by kind permission of Frederick Warne & Co. Published by Samuel French, London.

Whizziwig by Malorie Blackman (Viking, 1995), © Malorie Blackman, 1995. Reproduced by permission of Penguin Books Ltd and A. M. Heath Ltd. Published by Puffin Books, London.

The Wild Swans by Hans Andersen, adapted by Rona Laurie. Reproduced by permission of Rona Laurie.

BOYS 6-8

Beauty and the Beast by Nicholas Stuart Gray. Reproduced by permission of Dobson Books. Published by Samuel French, London.

Cider with Rosie by Laurie Lee, adapted by James Roose-Evans. Reproduced by permission of David Higham Associates Limited. Published by Samuel French, London.

GIRLS 9-10

The Princess and the Goblin stage adaptation © Stuart Paterson. From the book by George MacDonald. Reproduced by permission of Alan Brodie Representation Limited.

BOYS 9-10

Fantastic Mr Fox by Roald Dahl, adapted by Sally Reid. Reproduced by permission of David Higham Associates Limited. Published by Puffin Books, London.

Extract from *Flibberty and the Penguin* is reproduced by permission of Samuel French Ltd, 52 Fitzroy Street, London W1P 6JR to whom applications for public performance should be made.

James and the Giant Peach by Roald Dahl, adapted by Richard R. George. Reproduced by permission of David Higham Associates Ltd. Published by Puffin Books, London.

The Lion, the Witch and the Wardrobe by C.S. Lewis, dramatised by Adrian Mitchell. Reproduced by permission of Oberon Books Limited. Published by Oberon Books, London.

The Pied Piper by Adrian Mitchell. Reproduced by permission of The Peters, Fraser & Dunlop Group Limited. Published by Samuel French, London.

GIRLS 11-13

Charlotte's Web by E.B. White, adapted by Joseph Robinette. Copyright MCMLXXXIII by Joseph Robinette. Printed in the United States of America. All rights reserved. The scenes printed in this anthology are not to be used as acting scripts. All inquiries regarding performance rights should be addressed to Dramatic Publishing, 311 Washington St., Woodstock, IL60098. Phone: (815) 338-7170. Fax: (815) 338-8981. Published by The Dramatic Publishing Company, Illinois.

Invisible Friends by Alan Ayckbourn. Reproduced by permission of Faber & Faber Ltd. Published by Faber & Faber Ltd, London.

Extract edited from *Mr A's Amazing Maze Plays* by Alan Ayckbourn. Edited from Act II. Reproduced by permission of Faber & Faber Ltd. Published by Samuel French, London.

The Siege by Adrian Mitchell. Reproduced by permission of Oberon Books Limited. Published by Oberon Books, London.

Six Primroses Each by Ellen Dryden. Taken from *Six Primroses Each and Other Plays for Young Actors*. Reproduced by permission of First Writes Theatre Company Ltd. Published by First Writes Publications, London.

The Worst Witch by Jill Murphy, adapted by Paul Todd. Reproduced by permission of Paul Todd. Published by Puffin Books, London.

BOYS 11-13

The Children's Ward by Ellen Dryden. Taken from *Six Primroses Each and Other Plays for Young Actors*. Reproduced by permission of First Writes Theatre Company Ltd, Published by First Writes Publications, London.

Extract edited from *Ernie's Incredible Illucinations* by Alan Ayckbourn, from 'Plays Two'. Reproduced by permission of Faber & Faber Ltd. Published by Samuel French, London.

George's Marvellous Medicine © copyright 2000 Roald Dahl Nominee Ltd & Stuart Paterson. Adapted from Act I. All rights whatsoever in this play are strictly reserved and application for performance etc., must be made before rehearsal to Casarotto Ramsay & Associates Ltd., National House, 60-66 Wardour Street, London W1V 4ND. No performance may be given unless a licence has been obtained.

In Service by Ellen Dryden. Taken from *Six Primroses Each and Other Plays for Young Actors*. Reproduced by permission of First Writes Theatre Company Ltd. Published by First Writes Publications, London.

Jump For Your Life by Ken Whitmore. Reproduced by permission of The Agency (London) Ltd. © Ken Whitmore. First Published by Samuel French Ltd.

Just William by Richmal Crompton, taken from 'William and the Russian Prince'. Reproduced by permission of Macmillan. Published by Macmillan Children's Books, London.

The See-Saw Tree by David Wood. Copyright © David Wood, 1987, reproduced by permission of Amber Lane Press Ltd. Published by Amber Lane Press, Charlbury, Oxfordshire.

GIRLS 14-16

Easter by August Strindberg, translated by Peter Watts. Taken from *Three Plays by August Strindberg*. Copyright © Peter Watts, 1958. Reproduced by permission of Penguin Books Ltd. Published by Penguin Classics, London (1958).

Eclipse by Simon Armitage. Taken from *New Connections – New Plays for Young People*. Reproduced by permission of David Godwin Associates. Published by Faber & Faber Ltd, London.

In the Sweat by Naomi Wallace and Bruce McLeod. Taken from *New Connections – New Plays for Young People*. Reproduced by permission of The Rod Hall Agency Limited. Published by Faber & Faber Ltd, London.

The Power of the Dog by Ellen Dryden. Reproduced by permission of First Writes Theatre Company Ltd. Published by First Writes Publications, London.

The Secret Garden by Frances Hodgson Burnett, adapted by Thérèse Kitchin. Reproduced by permission of Thérèse Kitchin. Published by William Heinemann Ltd, Oxford.

The Witches © copyright 1993 Roald Dahl Nominee Ltd & David Wood. Adapted from Act I. Published by Samuel French, London. All rights whatsoever in this play are strictly reserved and application for performance etc., must be made before rehearsal to Casarotto Ramsay & Associates Ltd., National House, 60-66 Wardour Street, London W1V 4ND. No performance may be given unless a licence has been obtained.

BOYS 14-16

Chicken Soup with Barley by Arnold Wesker. Taken from *The Wesker Trilogy: Volume I.* Copyright © Arnold Wesker, 1959, 1960. Reproduced by permission of Penguin Books Ltd. First published by Penguin Books, 1964. Published by Samuel French, London.

Cider with Rosie by Laurie Lee, adapted by James Roose-Evans. Reproduced by permission of David Higham Associates Limited. Published by Samuel French, London.

Eclipse by Simon Armitage. Taken from *New Connections – New Plays for Young People.* Reproduced by permission of David Godwin Associates. Published by Faber & Faber Ltd, London.

In the Sweat by Naomi Wallace and Bruce McLeod. Taken from *New Connections – New Plays for Young People.* Reproduced by permission of The Rod Hall Agency Limited. Published by Faber & Faber Ltd, London.

'Master Harold' . . . and the Boys © Athol Fugard 1982. Reprinted from *'Master Harold' . . . and the Boys* by Athol Fugard (1982) by permission of Oxford University Press.

Extract from *The Winslow Boy* by Terence Rattigan. Reproduced by permission of Nick Hern Books, The Glasshouse, 49A Goldhawk Road, London W12 8QP. Tel: 020 8749 4953. Fax: 020 8746 2006. Email:info@nick-hernbooks.demon.co.uk. Published by Samuel French, London.

Every effort has been made to trace and acknowledge copyright owners. If any right has been omitted the publishers offer their apologies and will rectify this in subsequent editions following notification.